THE ALL-IN THING

MINISTRIES

C000008795

CONTENTS

Each **Section** contains an **Order of Service**, details on each element of the service (we call it the **Finer Details**!), a script for the **Story** and scripts for both **Drama** and **Puppet** sketches. Section 4 has a **Worksheet** too!

Concept design by Steve Squires ◉ **Cover design** by Beatroot Media ◉ **Inside design** by Sarah Joy at Random Panda **Printed** by Halcyon

This book uses designs based on icons from the Noun Project which are released under the Creative Commons Attribution (CC BY 3.0 US) licence. **www.thenounproject.com** ◉ *Arrows* by Juan Pablo Bravo • *Check box* by Dan Stack • *Hand* by Jakob Vogel • *Megaphone* by Lorena Salagre • *Mug* by Jacob Halton • *Pencil* by Grant Taylor • *Pray* by Cristiano Zoucas • *Speech bubble* by Mateo Zlatar • *Video player* by Felipe Santana

This book uses and gratefully acknowledges the following images. Those marked with an asterisk (*) are used in accordance with the Creative Commons Attribution (CC BY 2.0) licence. ◉ p9 *Food/drink 3* by Hans Thoursie (www.freeimages.com) • p13 *Three Kings* by Bartek Ambrozik (www.freeimages.com) • p18 *A-Mazing Game* by Jeff Prieb (www.freeimages.com) • p29 © Titovstudio | Dreamstime.com – *Book Pages In Heart Shape Photo* • p34 *Stoney Jenga** by Edward Crompton (www.flickr.com) • p45 *Chicks!** by Daniel Hall (www.flickr.com) • p50 *Old Wall* by ilker (www.freeimages.com) • p51, p115 *Notes On Wood 1* by Chris Greene (www.freeimages.com) • p61 *The Resurrection Of Jesus* by Bartek Ambrozik (www.freeimages.com) • p67 *Cross Variation* by Robert Aichinger (www.freeimages.com) • p77 *Project 365 #277: 041014 Dance Of The Flames** by Peter Brooks (www.flickr.com) • p83 *Candle* by VikaZayc (www.freeimages.com) • p93 *Bluewater Bridge* by Ry Young (www.freeimages.com) • p109 © Shaffandi | Dreamstime.com – *Silhouette Of Two Man Running At The Beach Photo* • p114 *Sewing Tools* by Kelsey Johnson (www.freeimages.com) • p115 *Füße Im Sand* by chris1961 (www.freeimages.com) • p125 *Visit From A Raven – Corvus Corax** by Ingrid Taylar (www.flickr.com) • p141 *In Remembrance** by Alosh Bennett (www.flickr.com) • p157 *Nativity** by Jeff Weese (www.flickr.com) • p162 *Lit Lanterns** by Ann (www.flickr.com)

Additional photography and craft by Sarah Joy, Hannah Kernthaler and Stephanie Laird

THANKS AND THINGS

We are so excited here at BIG Ministries to be launching **The All-In Thing**. We hope you are going to find it inspiring and useful! We've been dreaming of this project for years, and have been practicing, developing and fine-tuning it for the last seven years, and finally it is here.

There are so many people to thank, so many people who have given their time, energy and ideas to make this happen. I'm going to try to remember everyone…

First off, we have to thank God for being our inspiration, our focus and for making us all so different! Thank you God for giving us the amazing challenge of figuring out what it means to be together as church.

Thank you to the incredible BIG Ministries team (all of you!) who have been with us on this journey which has finally arrived at **The All-In Thing**. You're an amazing family to be part of.

Extra thanks go out to:

James Rubacki What a gifted script writer we have here… thanks to him for the incredible stories, sketches and for the inspiring creative input throughout the book.

Damian Herbert For stepping in, helping out, and for writing excellent sketches. For helping with asking the challenging questions and for being a great support.

Steve Squires Relentless care and creativity and passion for making sure this project is everything it had potential to be.

Sarah Joy Oh my word. Legend. Hours and hours of design and help, above and beyond the call of duty. It looks stunning.

Hannah Kernthaler Support, ideas, making things happen and being on the end of the phone to listen to out-loud processing!

Michael Whiteman For the excellent comedy puppet script writing debut.

YFC Family For all your input, ideas and support.

All at Elevation For believing in the project and for backing us to enable us to be able to pull it off!

The Proofreading Team Chris & Helen, Pete & Wendy and Pete Kernthaler. Well, it'd make much less sense without you!

THE NEW ALL-AGE RESOURCE THAT'S DESIGNED FOR EVERYONE!

At BIG Ministries, we're really passionate about **All-In worship.**

"What's **All-In worship**?", you may ask...

Well, the name **All-In** comes from a variety of ideas:

All-In = We're all in this together.

All-In = We're literally **all in** the same room.

All-In = We're giving it all we've got!

WHY DO ALL-IN?

Paul instructs us to be unified and united in love *(Philippians 2: 1-4)*, as a community of God's people *(1 Corinthians 12: 12-17)* all one in Christ Jesus *(Galatians 3: 28)* for His glory.

We believe there should definitely be times where we come together as the whole church, regardless of age, ability, gender or personal preferences, and be united in love as a community of God's people. We do this because we love Him and want to worship Him together, learning about Him, learning from Him, and learning from one another too.

It should be a beautiful time where every person makes sacrifices and everybody prefers one another.

It should also be a time that is good and a time when everyone can have the opportunity to genuinely worship our awesome God!

WHY NOT 'ALL-AGE'?

When planning an 'all-age' service we tend to think in terms of age groups. The standard planning process is to make sure the children can engage and the adults can engage (and unfortunately, the young people can often get forgotten about – let's be honest, they are a bit complicated!). So when choosing an element for the service, you might think of a two-year-old, a 22-year-old, a 52-year-old and a 72-year-old and consider if that element is suitable for them. If it isn't, we try to add something in to make that element work.

The problem with this approach can be that, in practice, 'all-age' ends up being 'no age'. An act of worship aimed at a four-year-old is unlikely to be that accessible for a 74-year-old and vice versa. The challenge to find one thing that enables everyone to engage with God in the same way is perhaps an impossible task.

For example, I am a children's worker, but I don't want to join in with a song that's aimed at four-year-olds, or be forced to do actions by an over-enthusiastic children's worker bouncing around at the front of church. I struggle to engage with something that is called a 'children's talk' and I don't want to pray to God to say sorry for the naughty things I've done. I am not four, and I am not 58, or 72 or 17... I am 33. I'm a different age from the majority of people. I am however an extrovert, I am an out-loud processor, I am someone who can't sit still, I learn by doing and I can't concentrate on one thing for more than about five minutes. I love music, but not always singing, I love to talk, I love to have fun, I don't do well with long periods of silence or reflection, I struggle with listening to long talks. That's just who I am. But I am a valid member of the Body of Christ in my uniqueness.

And that's just me. If you multiply that out across a large congregation and take account of every person's unique qualities and preferences it's no wonder that this all-age approach doesn't always work well. It can often result in a service that is very childish, as we seek to accommodate the very youngest, or it can become very 'adult' as we don't want to compromise the 'worship experience' of the older members of the congregation. Unfortunately this often means that everyone struggles to engage. Also, sadly, all-age worship can become exclusively focused on families, meaning that people without children, or young people, or people who are beyond the young family stage, can feel excluded and struggle with being forced to engage with a children's action song that they can't relate to.

I've had interesting conversations with people who claim to be passionate about all-age worship but don't want anything to 'interrupt' the flow of worship – which really means they don't want to compromise their standard three songs in a row. I've also, at the other extreme, had conversations with over-zealous children's workers who get frustrated that their church won't engage with bouncy, high energy (sometimes silly) children's songs, and that their vicar needs convincing to make the services all about the children.

There must be a better way.

We believe there is. And it's called **All-In**.

AN ALL-IN ANALOGY

Everyone coming together as a Church Family should be the most amazing and uplifting time; a time of encouragement and learning together, a time of worship and prayer and a time of 'being' a true, diverse family. It is devastating, then, that all-age worship just doesn't seem to work.

I truly believe that God loves it when we come together, when we sacrifice our preferences and when we strive to facilitate others in their worship and spiritual growth. What do I mean by this? Well, how about an analogy that we can all hopefully relate to...

Think about Christmas day. What a perfect time to spend as a family. The beauty of Christmas is that (in an ideal world) the whole family gathers in one location to be united in their celebrations. During the day there will be times when the whole family (everyone, whatever their age, ability, differences or shoe size) all do something together. Probably when the food happens! Everyone takes the time to be with each other; to sit around, enjoy good food and spend time chatting and enjoying each other's company.

There will also be times during the day when there will be a degree of separation – some people will be having a coffee and an after dinner mint while some will be investigating new toys, some will be watching *The Snowman* and others might be playing a game on their new tablet. Although there are separate activities going on, the family is all still together even though they may not all be doing exactly the same thing all day.

The great thing about the celebration of Christmas is that the family is gathered, differences are put aside in favour of being together, and time is invested in relationships with no agenda or 'jobs' to be done. There is inevitably compromise from everyone, especially for the 'together times', and that is what makes it good, and what makes it such a beautiful scene. Love for each other is the priority.

We like to think of **All-In** in a similar way.

A worship gathering is intended to build relationships with God and with each other. The gathered people will have moments of complete unity and togetherness as they engage with a Bible story, or sing a song of worship. There will be moments of worship where the focus of the worship (Jesus) is the unifying element, even though the vehicle for the worship (singing, art, activity, reading, thinking, writing, talking and more!) may be different.

Can we really begin to think and act as if we are a real family?

A DIFFERENT WAY OF THINKING

We are all different, and yet we all have a uniting force – worshipping God. John Drane's definition is of "us responding to all that God is with all that we are."

Everything that makes me 'me' is completely different from everything that makes you 'you'. It's not about me being a different age (some might say I am actually very similar to an eight-year-old), it's about me being a person whom God has created as a unique individual.

So we're proposing a drastic change in thinking. We should stop thinking about different age groups and instead think about the different needs of people – who are all different!

So, let's bear in mind:

Non-readers in the congregation ◉ People with **limited mobility** ◉ People who **can't bring themselves to sing in public** ◉ People who have a **visual impairment** ◉ People who **need to not sit still** ◉ People with a **hearing impairment** ◉ People who are **creative** ◉ People who are **thinkers** ◉ People who **need to talk** ◉ People who **like to be alone** ◉ People who **love to sing** ◉ People who **like to be still** ◉ People who **learn by seeing** ◉ People who **learn by doing** ◉ People who **learn by hearing** ◉ **Extroverts** ◉ **Introverts** ◉ **Writers** ◉ **Techies** ◉ **Artists** ◉ **Males** ◉ **Females** ◉ ... and all the rest!

If we shift our thinking and move away from our standard "this is how church works" or "this is what a church service has to look like" mindset, we should be able to create a gathering that is truly for everyone and is truly **All-In**.

It's risky, it's exciting... and it can be beautiful!

WHAT MAKES IT ALL-IN

There are three foundational elements to bear in mind when we're thinking of **All-In** and making our services truly for everyone.

Hospitality

When do you ever go and visit a friend or family member and not get offered a drink or something to eat when you arrive? Why is it that in church mostly we have to wait until the end of the service to get coffee and a biscuit? (I know that's not always the case, but it happens more often than not. I've even been to a church service where there is no coffee. NO COFFEE?!).

The reality is that by the time you get to Church you've either been up for hours and could do with a drink, or you've just dragged yourself out of bed to make it on time and could do with a drink and possibly even breakfast! Jesus spent a lot of His time eating with people. It's a very normal thing to do, it's a necessary and yet potentially wonderful element of life. It's relaxed, there's no formality to abide by, and it's nice to have a decent cup of coffee (or tea) and a nice bit of cake.

People on the welcome team need to have the gift of hospitality and be naturally welcoming. But it mustn't stop there. The best **All-In** services are where that hospitality continues throughout the whole service. Think about what makes a good host and bring that into your service. My little boy is three and he has an amazing gift of hospitality that I can learn from! When someone new comes to our house he takes them by the hand and introduces them to everyone in our family, shows them where the lounge is, where the kitchen is, that there's a toilet in here (and the light switch is on the outside) and therefore instantly makes them feel welcome by helping them to know how it works in our household.

Throughout the service we can continue to help people feel at ease by simply explaining what is happening, why we are doing what we're doing and who can do it.

There needs to be freedom for people to engage in ways that work for them and feel like there is space for movement (without the expectation of getting stares from people). Think about the freedom a crawling baby has and the way that everyone accepts that they need to keep moving and so it's OK for them to be crawling. Those who struggle to sit still and need to keep moving in order to stick with the programme and concentrate on what's happening should surely be granted the same acceptance.

So firstly, and crucially, we need to practice abundant hospitality.

Ritual

Pantomime. Love it or hate it, there's no denying it works. Everyone knows there are certain things that always happen, and everyone knows how to respond. It's full of great story, humour and ritual. "Oh no it isn't!"

Pantomime facilitates involvement because everyone knows how to respond – we have to know the rituals. And this is often where we fail in church and people can feel disempowered because the rituals are complicated, unexplained or unfamiliar.

Ritualisation in **All-In** means having things that happen every time so that people know what to expect, such as always starting with the same 'gathering' song. Following the same format for the service can relax people as they know what to expect next. It also means explaining things clearly and simply, setting up expectations about how things are going to work.

All-In does not need to be reduced to entertainment or to something that's completely informal, and that's not what I'm implying with the link to pantomime. It's just that we need to think completely differently and lead this new style of worship in a new way. Just explain it rather than expecting people to know what's happening or how it works.

This explaining of ritual and making things accessible for people without any expectations of them is going to naturally make our church more accessible to those 'unchurched' who might enter our doors to the smell of fresh coffee and croissants (!). How exciting if church could be a place where everybody feels like they belong and can be who they truly are?

Ritualisation coupled with hospitality should create a brilliant relaxed space where not only can people worship God freely, but difficult issues can be explored. It makes a space safe, and people will feel sufficiently comfortable to be real and open.

Joy

Why is it that we're not always first described as joyful people? If someone is describing you, would they use the word joyful? I know that's a challenge to me. I think I'm too serious sometimes about everything because I don't want to look silly or have people think something other than "she's amazing" about me.

Being full of joy means that no matter what's happening around us (good or bad) we can be positive, happy even, because we know who we belong to, we know that God is good and we're still people who can have fun. Especially when we're with a group of people who we know and love. Surely church should be a place where we can have fun, be full of joy and help people who are struggling with joy to be overcome by it!

Of course, I'm not saying there's no place for the serious or contemplation, there absolutely is, but we don't need to be 'well-behaved' (whatever that is) or 'solemn' all the time. That's not how Jesus behaved and neither should we.

Let's be joyful people, it's an attractive quality. If we are full of God's joy, people will be drawn to us and our **All-In Worship** will be uplifting and inspiring.

So with the foundation of hospitality, ritual and joy, we can look at the two main ways we engage with God and each other during **All-In Worship**.

❶ Together times

Everyone being together doing the same activity has its challenges, but it's absolutely crucial. The majority of our church life can be spent in separation: children's and youth groups, ladies' groups, men's breakfasts, toddler groups, leadership meetings, planning groups, worship team meals and so many more. These times are so important, and I'm absolutely all for having sessions that meet a specific group's needs, but having moments together is what makes us so unique as a 'movement' and also what gives us the biggest challenge.

Within an **All-In Service** there are a lot of moments where we are in the same room and potentially engaging with God in a variety of ways. But it's vital that we maintain the together-together times! We must set the foundation for our learning and our worship together to then engage with that foundation and with God in potentially different ways.

The things we do together are foundational to our service: looking at the Bible and exploring the main points to think on for the service (in ways that are interactive and engaging). There might also be a time where we are singing the same song or woshipping together as a sign of our unity and love for each other and for God.

❷ All-In Sync

This is the potentially messy and exciting (!) part of the **All-In Service**. This is the part that's modelled on the Christmas day afternoon example where we are all together, but possibly engaging in Christmas in slightly differing ways.

So now people can engage in worship in the way that makes most sense to them. We are **All-In Sync** as we are focused on one specific goal – to worship God and to respond to who He is – but we are not all necessarily engaging in the same way. Some could be singing, some creating a masterpiece with paper and glue, others sitting and thinking on their own, some discussing the topic for the day, some writing, some moving around, some serving others by preparing something for later in the service and other things too!

One major positive thing about the **All-In Sync** times is that no-one is being forced to engage in a certain way. I know a lot of people who struggle with All-age worship particularly because they feel like they are being "made to do action songs". With these **All-In Sync** times, people can choose what activities they engage with – with no particular requirement to engage in a certain way.

This is the part that is going to feel the most different to a 'normal' service of worship where we all are led in the same activities for the duration of the service. You may decide that it would be too much to start this immediately and that you would benefit more from a gradual introduction of **All-In Sync** times.

Within the plans in this book there are some simple **All-In Sync** times with only one or two options for people to choose their method of engagement. For example, there could be a song led from the front while there is the opportunity to also be involved in an activity where you are able to sit and think or pray about some relevant Bible passages. These might be a good starting point to introduce this new approach to your congregation.

In the longer term what's exciting is that we may not need to introduce this sort of freedom. People may no longer need to be given permission to engage in a way that makes sense to them. If we truly embrace **Hospitality, Ritual** and **Joy,** then the **All-In Times** may just happen naturally as people feel free in worship.

ALL-IN WORSHIP

I really believe we need to start thinking away from ages and think about abilities, restrictions and differences for people. Then we can begin to help people feel comfortable in their own skin at church and worship God as they are, even if they struggle with singing or have never been in a church before or can't sit still!

So I hope you have caught a bit of the vision for **All-In**. I'm excited! I hope you are too. It's new, it's a shift in thinking and it could potentially change the way that church works as a whole, not just for all-age services.

Ten themed sessions of **All-In Worship** are included in this resource, but before you get stuck in there's a few more practicalities to consider.

Jo Squires

PRACTICALITIES
FOR RECURRING ITEMS
(in order of appearance in your order of service!)

WELCOME

This should be a time of generous hospitality. Real coffee, nice tea, real milk and good food – breakfast foods or cakes or pastries are always a winner.

Make sure you provide nice cold drinks too, and even think about a microwave for those who might need to warm milk or food for babies, as well as gluten-free and dairy-free snacks.

It's always a good idea to make food zones like this nut-free, then it's just not an issue should someone with a nut allergy come to the service.

During this welcome make sure there are seats available (some people won't be able to stand for a long time) as well as clearly labelled Welcome People (!) who can tell people what's happening / be really friendly.

To avoid the danger of spillage of hot drinks onto busy small people, perhaps provide a toys area or a space in another room where there are big toys out or even just space to run around safely!

SING

This opening song is to be used as a gathering song, to call people together from the coffee / cake time and should be the same every week. We have used *Everybody's Welcome** (Nigel Hemming) as our choice as it is a great scene-setter for the whole of the rest of the service.

It's good to announce it, but people will gradually learn that this song means it's time to gather in the main church area.

PRAYER  PSALM

Every service outline has a psalm as the opening element.

The concept of this is to help people engage with the scripture. Read the psalm through and then invite people to join in with the psalmist's instructions, if they are able. This should result in people singing / clapping / cheering etc. as the psalmist asks them to!

Follow this with an opening prayer and the service is ready to start.

CREATE

This creative act is for everyone to do together. Whoever leads this from the front must speak clearly and be confident with what they are doing.

Ideally do a 'giant' version of the activity. So use a massive piece of paper so people can see what you're doing, or a giant pipe cleaner if that's what's being used! Ideally with a live video link up to a screen which then makes it easier for people to see.

 There are instructional videos at *bigministries.co.uk/theallinthing* which can teach you how to do them.

ACT STORY

Scripts for the stories are provided for you. We recommend using these with all the actors and props involved because it makes the story come to life and is a lot of fun to be part of.

This is a great way to potentially get different groups from the church involved – you could give the story to the youth group to produce one week, and then to the men's breakfast another week to plan and perform. Could be very entertaining!

TELL

The talks are all really short, deliberately so. They are to make a simple point that everyone can take home. There are many other mediums of communication throughout the service that people can take different things from, and the **All-In Sync** section is really where people can explore what God might be saying to them today.

ACT

Every service has the option of a puppet script or a drama sketch. This is really for you to choose which you think you can do better. Feel free of course to write your own or adapt it for your use. We fully appreciate that it's a lot of work to produce these which is why we have written them for you to use.

ALL-IN SYNC

This is the most exciting part of the service!

Now, it could be that your church main room is massive and flexible and it's easy for you to set up all these zones within the one room. But it could also be that you just don't have space to set them all up and we do recognise that. We have a few suggestions:

- ◉ Make it a slightly longer 'slot' and use any other spaces in your building that you have. Perhaps use the main room for the **SING** zone and another couple of zones – like **DISCUSS** and **WRITE** – and send **THINK, MOVE** and **CREATE**, for example, to other rooms.

- ◉ Don't do all of the zones, just do what you have space for.

- ◉ Make most of the zones 'non-zones' and provide the equipment for people to do the activity where they are or move to get said equipment they need and sit wherever they can. Provide clip boards and paper for **WRITE**, ear defenders and cushions for **THINK**. Provide tangle-toys or smaller contained physical activity for **MOVE**. You will need to provide an area for the **DISCUSS** zone if possible, because that's not really doable on your own!

RESPOND

This section of the service will often use the **CREATE** from earlier in the service to help people engage and respond to God in a physical way – giving up the thing they have created or adapting it in response to God and the theme.

OTHER THINGS TO REMEMBER

Introducing songs and parallel activities

The introduction of elements is crucial to their success. We must always introduce in a 'normal' way, not making activities 'for' anyone in-particular.

An example: *"We're going to worship God for His big-ness now – there is a song you can sing with us, with actions if you'd like to join in with them and there is also a creative activity happening over here too… Let's celebrate how big God is together. Stand with me if you're able."*

Hospitality

Don't forget to explain things and make people feel safe to be involved in ways that make sense to them throughout the service. Have people who are clued up as to what's going on in the service 'around' to help people who might need a bit of guidance.

Perhaps have some orders of service printed out for people who need to know what's happening, along with magnifying glasses, or in large print.

Be yourself and be a worshipper

If you are leading the service, just be yourself – don't try to be all over-enthusiastic or something you are not. Be enthusiastic, but be true to who you are too. Engage in everything yourself and see this as an opportunity to worship as you lead others.

DRAMA, PUPPETS
AND CHARACTER BIOGRAPHIES

DRAMA

Before you read through any of the drama sketches, we thought it'd be helpful for you to know a little bit about how they work and how the characters should be portrayed, as this will affect how the drama is communicated.

The scripts' intentions are (usually) to make light of a Biblical truth. On the whole this is done through our two characters, Ben and Jen, being very silly. They usually get things very wrong and do things in ways that they shouldn't be done – hopefully helping us to see the way that things should be done and how we should be as God's church. Some of the sketches can make a stand-alone point, whereas others will need some explanation or teaching drawn from them afterwards.

CHARACTER BIOGRAPHIES

Ben

Ben is quite a loud and strange character. He loves getting up to mischief, with his two favourite things in the world being water pistols and fizzy pop. Ben is quite clumsy – fast to act but slow to think. His temper is fairly short and he usually takes this out on his best friend, Jen (or on the audience watching). He often gets carried away with his own thoughts and can be tough to speak to when he's made his mind up about something. He does have a sensitive side though and is eager to please, which is why he gets so frustrated when he gets things wrong.

Jen

Jen is ever so slightly brighter than Ben and fairly quick witted. Jen is a bit quicker to see when things are going wrong and, now and again, can see the right way of doing things. She sees herself as responsible for Ben but gets annoyed with Ben's persistent mistakes and temper tantrums. Just like Ben, Jen gets carried away with her own thoughts and can take things too far, especially when she's trying to get Ben to go along with her plans. The majority of the time, Jen is at hand to either calm Ben down, to stop Ben from offending the audience, and to apologise on Ben's behalf.

We recommend that you read through the scripts with one another before performing, until you're familiar with them. You can either perform these scripts word for word or, as you get more comfortable with them, feel free to ad-lib and add your own interpretation into the scripts. Allow your character to develop as you see appropriate and make sure you get some really fun colourful outfits for each of them. We also recommend coming up with a name for each of the characters. (Let's be honest, Ben and Jen aren't really the most creative names...)

PUPPETS

Before you read through the puppet script, it would most likely be helpful to you if you knew a little bit about the characters, as this will affect how you read and communicate the script. So, there are up to three characters in the scripts – the intention is that you will make up your own names for these characters, but we've just gone with Jack, Jill and Alex for now to make things simple. Jack and Jill are the two puppets and Alex is a human (someone who doesn't have a puppet attached to their arm) who interacts with the two puppets.

CHARACTER BIOGRAPHIES

Jack

Jack is loud, full of energy, quick to speak and slow to think. He's easily confused and isn't the smartest of puppets, which often frustrates him a great deal, although he does try very hard to get his head around some pretty big subject matters. Jack is quick to answer back and has a very short attention span. He likes jam sandwiches, computer games and sleeping in in the morning, but gets annoyed at his mum waking him up for school. He can sometimes have a low opinion of himself, especially when put up against his best mate, Jill, who is 'super intelligent', but he gets carried away with himself when he does actually understand something or knows the answer to a question.

Jill

Jill is kind, clever, sarcastic and quick to show off. Jill likes to think of herself as 'the most cleverest person in the world'. It's fair to say, she does know a fair bit, but she isn't half as clever as she thinks she is. Jill will usually comment on Jack's 'pea sized brain' but does try to take care of him and teach him (usually in a very sarcastic way). In fact, she's sarcastic most of the time and will tend to form a running commentary for her own amusement. Her intentions are good most of the time. When Jill doesn't know the answer to something, rather than owning up to it, she'll usually cover it up with some wise and cheeky comments. Jill gets on very well with Jack but does like to think of herself as superior to him.

Alex

Alex is the human in the situation. Alex will usually show up when either Jack or Jill call for him / her or when Alex overhears some kind of argument between Jack and Jill – which is fairly often. Alex is the teacher and is very sensible, kind and patient. Alex attempts to help Jack and Jill think things through for themselves and together they all come to some kind of conclusion.

So, these are our characters. We recommend that you read through the scripts with one another before performing, until you're familiar with them. You can either read these scripts word for word or, as you get more comfortable with them, feel free to let your puppet develop into its own character – add some of your own humour, ad-lib a little, mix things up a bit... but don't get too carried away, as your arm might fall asleep.

PERSEVERANCE

1

THEME

The overarching theme for this service is **with God's help we can persevere.**

It might seem strange to be talking about perseverance as the first theme in a book, but it's so important. Walking with God is the best thing, but it's also a complicated journey. Sometimes it's really, really hard and we need to figure out how to keep going.

STORY

The Magi went on an **epic journey** to get to see Jesus.

Their journey took them through all sorts of trials, probably travelling through interesting weather, not having anywhere to sleep (which, being wealthy men would have been a challenge, I'm sure) and then there was the challenge of having to deal with (and later, avoid) the fairly evil King Herod!

I believe they made it through this challenge because of three reasons: ❶ They had God's help; ❷ They had each other; ❸ They wholeheartedly believed in their cause.

IDEAS

This service would fit nicely into the service of **Epiphany** if you are based in a church that follows the Church Calendar.

Otherwise it would work really well for a service in January, setting the scene for the rest of the year.

ORDER OF SERVICE

3 MINS — **INTRODUCTION / WELCOME**

3 MINS — **SING** *Everybody's Welcome*

2 MINS — **PRAY** Psalm 47: 1–7

4 MINS

SING
Awesome Is The Lord Most High

WRITE
Praise Wall

4 MINS — **CREATE** Making stars

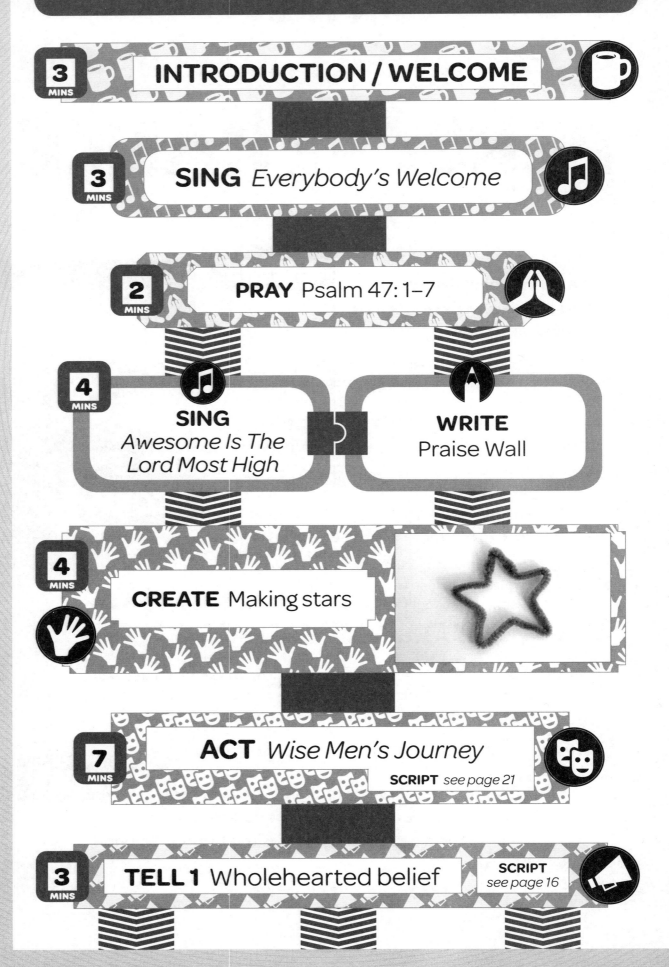

7 MINS — **ACT** *Wise Men's Journey*
SCRIPT *see page 21*

3 MINS — **TELL 1** Wholehearted belief
SCRIPT *see page 16*

4 MINS

SING *Strong And Brave*

THINK God's promises

MOVE Actions

OPTION A

4 MINS

ACT – DRAMA Perseverance through adversity

SCRIPT *see page 24*

OPTION B

ACT – PUPPETS How can I keep my eyes fixed on Jesus?

SCRIPT *see page 26*

3 MINS

TELL 2 Keep focused on Jesus

SCRIPT *see page 17*

15 MINS

ALL-IN SYNC ALL-IN SYNC ALL-IN SYNC

SING 3-4 songs about persevering

CREATE Tricky joint picture

MOVE Obstacles

WRITE Short story about perseverance

DISCUSS Issues concerning persevering with Jesus

THINK How to persevere with Jesus

3 MINS

RESPOND Make a star mobile. Will you persevere?

4 MINS

SING *To God Be The Glory*

MOVE Sign language

MOVE Ribbons / flags

THE FINER DETAIL

SING ▶ WRITE

SING

Lead the congregation in a song about how big and awesome God is, e.g. *Awesome Is The Lord Most High**.

WRITE

A large piece of paper with the word PRAISE written on it on the floor or on a wall for people to draw or write their praise to God. Also provide clipboards and paper for those unable to access the large piece.

CREATE ◉ STARS

There are three varying options for making stars:

The Trickiest option Origami map stars

You need: Squares from old map paper – two per person
Glue or double sided sticky tape – one per row

▶ Learn to make an origami star.
www.bigministries.co.uk/theallinthing.

Lead everyone in creating their stars.

The Zero-Prep option Pipe cleaner stars

You need: Pipe cleaners – one per person

Practice how to make a star from a pipe-cleaner.

Lead everyone in creating their stars.

The Easy-to-Do option Foil stars

You need: Pieces of foil – one per person

Lead everyone in squashing their foil to become a star shape.

TELL 1 ◉ WHOLEHEARTED BELIEF

We have just heard the story of the Wise Men and their journey to meet Jesus.

They would have been travelling for a good deal of time. The general consensus amongst scholars is that they finally arrived with Jesus, not twelve days after his birth (as is generally celebrated today), but up to two years later! That's a long time to be following a star on a bit of a whim that there could be something good at the end of their journey!

They were Wise Men – they were the people that others would look to for help in tricky situations.

They were Wise Men – people who others would watch and follow their example.

They were Wise Men – men who truly and wholeheartedly believed that this star was important.

They were Wise Men who were on to something – they got stuck in and got on with it, no matter what. They persevered, and with God's help and the help of their friends, they made it to their destination.

What these Wise Men believed in made a difference to their life.

SING ▶ THINK ▶ MOVE

SING

*Strong And Brave****** – this song is on *The All-In Thing Songs* CD.

THINK

Spend some time thinking about God's promises. Provide Bibles for people, also invite them to search online on their phones for verses or quotes about God's promises

MOVE

▶ There are actions for the song – see *www.bigministries.co.uk/theallinthing.*

TELL 2 ◉ KEEP FOCUSED ON JESUS

Hebrews 12: 1–3 *(The Message)* **says this:**

Do you see what this means – all these pioneers who blazed the way, all these veterans cheering us on? It means we'd better get on with it. Strip down, start running – and never quit! No extra spiritual fat, no parasitic sins. Keep your eyes on Jesus, who both began and finished this race we're in. Study how he did it. Because he never lost sight of where he was headed – that exhilarating finish in and with God – he could put up with anything along the way: Cross, shame, whatever. And now he's there, in the place of honour, right alongside God. When you find yourselves flagging in your faith, go over that story again, item by item, that long litany of hostility he plowed through. That will shoot adrenaline into your souls!

Jesus never once lost sight of his goal. Jesus kept going and continued in His journey to that goal even when it was tough. He knew that He could do it – He had the support of His Father and the support of His friends, the disciples.

We can learn from Jesus, and His example of perseverance. Let us strive to keep going for God, knowing that He will help us, and let us strive to help others along on their journey of perseverance with God too.

As we move into our various activities now, let's keep Jesus in focus.

THE FINER DETAIL PERSEVERANCE

SING

Sing a few songs related to following Jesus no matter what.

Blessed Be Your Name
Beth Redman, Matt Redman

Be Thou My Vision
Dallan Forgaill

You Never Let Go
Matt Redman

I Have Decided To Follow Jesus
Unknown

Be The Centre
Michael Frye

*God Is Our Strength And Refuge
(Dambusters)* Richard Bewes

Hosanna (Praise Is Rising)
Brenton Brown, Paul Baloche

*Shout To The Lord (My Jesus,
My Saviour)* Darlene Zschech

Everlasting God (Strength Will Rise)
Brenton Brown, Ken Riley

Copyright details for these songs can be found on page 28.

CREATE

You need a giant piece of paper (on the wall or on the floor) with a short line in the middle.

You also need a list of simple things to draw. (e.g. star, TV, bed, window, map, flower, person, house, church)

We are going to persevere in this **CREATE** challenge – you take it in turns to turn the line (and then the previous drawing) into the next item on the list. It will probably be tricky, but others can help with ideas and encouragement.

Have available some spare pieces of paper and pens for independent free drawing or colouring.

During the activity, or when the drawing is finished, talk about:

What helped you draw the complicated things?

How can we keep going as a Christian even when it's tough?

MOVE

Set up a mini obstacle course. Challenge those who are part of this activity to get through the obstacle course as quickly as they can. Make the challenge more difficult by balancing a beanbag on their head or trying it blindfolded.

If you don't have the space, you could use some table-top obstacle course game like *Screwball Scramble*.

During the activity, or when people have completed the game, talk about:

What is it that makes you keep going?

How can we keep going as a Christian even when it's tough?

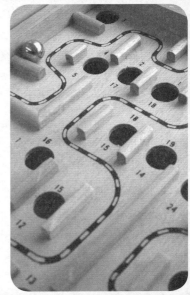

WRITE

Make sure you have some nice writing paper, nice pens and Bibles available.

"Write a short story about perseverance."

DISCUSS

Someone leading the discussion is ideal – here are some questions to get you started.

Discuss:

What do you believe in? Does it make a difference to your life?

How does believing in Jesus impact the way you live?

What makes it tough to follow Jesus?

Can we help each other? How?

How can we follow Jesus' example? He is God!

THINK

Make available: Bibles, cushions, ear defenders, paper, pens and even mp3 players with headphones.

Think about:

What do you believe in? Does it make a difference to your life?

How does believing in Jesus impact the way you live?

What makes it tough to follow Jesus?

Can we help each other? How?

RESPOND

We are going to use the stars that people made earlier in the service for the response.

Invite people to think for a minute about whether they are ready to follow Jesus, no matter what the cost. Are you ready to persevere for Him? Are you ready to help others on their journey too?

Create a 'washing line' for the stars. Provide pegs for people to attach their stars. Make sure there is someone available to collect stars from those who are unable to get to the line.

After giving people a minute to think about the questions, invite them to come and add their star to the line as their commitment to persevering for God.

Pray for us to be able to persevere and for God to help us to do that.

PERSEVERANCE THE FINER DETAIL

SING MOVE MOVE

SING

To God Be The Glory* – this song is on *The All-In Thing Songs* CD.

MOVE

For sign language for the chorus of this song, see *www.bigministries.co.uk/theallinthing*.

MOVE

Provide ribbons or flags for those who find them helpful in their worship.

PRAY

It's not on the order of service, but do close the service with prayer!

ACT ● STORY

WISE MEN'S JOURNEY ● MATTHEW 2: 1-12

Characters:

- Narrator 1
- Narrator 2
- Mary
- Joseph
- Jesus as a baby
- Shepherd 1
- Shepherd 2
- Wise Man 1
- Wise Man 2
- Wise Man 3
- The Star (a person dressed as a star)
- King Herod

You will need:

- Three gifts – gold, frankincense, myrrh

Teach the audience these **trigger words** *before reading the story:*

Wise Men
Say **"hmmm"**, *and stroke your chin, just like a wise person deep in thought.*

Travelled / travelling
Say **"hup, 2, 3, 4"**, *and if you want to you can march on the spot as you say it.*

Star
Hold up your star and say **"twinkle, twinkle, little star"** *as fast as you can.*

[Enter stage – Mary, Joseph, baby Jesus, Shepherd 1 and 2]

Narrator 1: Jesus had been born in Bethlehem and, while He lay there in the animal's feeding trough, people came to visit Him – including some shepherds and some **Wise Men** who **travelled** from far away in the East.

Shepherd 1: Erm… I can't see any **Wise Men** here.

Shepherd 2: No **Wise Men** here? Speak for yourself. I was second in my field in leadership skills. First place went to Terry… He's a clever little lamb, bless his woollen socks.

> Someone dressed as Terry the lamb could walk past reading a physics text book.

Shepherd 1: Like I said… I can't see any **Wise Men** here.

Narrator 2: Well… where are the **Wise Men** then?

Shepherds and Mary and Joseph: We don't know!

[Exit stage – Shepherds and Mary and Joseph, mumbling to one another as they walk off… "I don't know where they are. Do you know where they are? No, I don't know where they are…"]

Narrator 1: I guess they must have been **travelling** from further away than we thought… Oh look! What a coincidence. Here they are now.

[Enter stage – Wise men following a person dressed as the star]

Wise Man 1: Which one are we following again?

Wise Man 2 and 3: *[Pointing at the star]* THAT ONE! That BIG **star**!

Wise Man 1: Really? Are you sure that's not just a person dressed up as a **star**?

Wise Man 2: That's preposterous.

Wise Man 3: Ridiculous.

Narrator 2: And so, the **Wise Men** continued on their way to find Jesus, the one who had been born King of the Jews.

[Wise men and the star make their way through the audience and back to the stage]

> As they walk through the audience, the Wise Men could hand out personalised business cards to people they walk past.

Narrator 1: They **travelled** long and far, until… arriving in Jerusalem, the **Wise Men** began to ask the people, "Where is the one who has been born the King of the Jews?"

Wise Men 1, 2 and 3: *[Facing audience]* Where is the one who has been born King of the Jews?

[Enter stage – King Herod. King Herod and the Wise Men and the Star all huddle in together]

Narrator 2: Now, King Herod soon got news of this 'new king' and arranged a secret meeting with the **Wise Men**. But he had his own agenda.

King Herod: So, I've heard that… *[Looking at the star]* Sorry, who are you?

Star: I'm the **star**.

King Herod: Would you leave please. This doesn't concern you. *[The Star walks away with head hung low]* As I was saying, I've heard that the 'King of the Jews' has been born! *[Half hearted celebration]*… Whoopee, yeah, woop… So, when you find Him, could you pleeeease let me know? I cannot wait to kill Him… meet Him!

[Exit stage – King Herod]

Wise Man 2: What a nice guy.

Wise Man 3: Indeed.

Wise Man 1: I'm sure I heard him say he wants to kill the baby?

Wise Man 2: Preposterous.

Wise Man 3: Ridiculous.

Narrator 1: And so, the **Wise Men** followed the **star**…

[The star comes back excitely, standing tall, and leads them around the audience again. While they are wandering around, Mary, Joseph and Jesus enter stage with the baby, Jesus.]

Narrator 2: They followed and **travelled**,

Narrator 1: … and **travelled** and followed,

Narrator: 2: ... Until finally, the **star** led them to arrive at the exact place where Jesus lay.

Narrator 1: And when they found Him, they worshipped Him, and presented Him with gifts.

Wise Man 1: My King, accept my humble gift of Frankincense.

Wise Man 2: My Lord, accept my humble gift of Myrrh.

Wise Man 3: My Lord and King, accept my humble gift of... *[cough cough]* Gold.

Wise Men 1 and 2: Gold!?

Wise Man 1: We had a spending limit and you go and show us up by getting gold!?

Wise Man 3: Please, gentleman. Now is not the time.

Narrator 2: And so, the **Wise Men**, having **travelled** from afar, having followed a **star**, having spoken to King Herod, having found Jesus and having presented Him with gifts, worshipped Him until night came and their beds called.

[Everyone lies down to sleep... briefly] [Pause]

You could play some sound effects of night owls and crickets here. Then you could wake the Wise Men up with the sound of an alarm clock.

Narrator 1: Waking in the morning, each of the **Wise Men** sat up at the same time.

Narrator 2: They looked at each other, eyes open wide.

Narrator 1: Then they said...

Wise man 1, 2 and 3: *[Altogether]* I had a dream! You had a dream? What did you dream? That we should not tell King Herod where to find Jesus! ... No way! Me too!

Wise man 1: I knew he was bad news.

Narrator 1: And so, the **Wise Men** gathered their belongings and **travelled** back to their country via a different route, avoiding King Herod and his men.

[The wise men begin walking off and the star follows them]

Wise man 1: *[Talking to the star]* Where do you think you're going?

Star: With you guys?

Wise man 2: But, the journey's done.

Wise man 3: We don't need you any more. We've no need for a **star**.

[Star begins to walk the opposite way, head hung low]

Wise man 1: Oh, come on then. Follow us.

[Star turns and smiles and follows the Wise Men as they exit stage]

Wise man 1, 2, 3, and Star: Bye everyone...

Narrator 2: The end.

ACT ● DRAMA

PERSEVERANCE THROUGH ADVERSITY

**Ben and Jen are about to compete
in an obstacle course race.**

Prior to the sketch you will need to set up a mini course on stage –
a few things to go under and go over and go through.

You will need:
- ◉ A referee
- ◉ A whistle
- ◉ A trophy
- ◉ Several people to discourage Ben and Jen from winning
- ◉ Water pistols
- ◉ Obstacles for the obstacle course

Ben: Jen, you will never beat me at this challenge. I've been practicing. Nothing will stop me.

Jen: OK, Ben.

Ben: I've been working out, as I'm sure you can tell.

[Ben flexes his muscles]

Jen: I can't. But OK.

Ben: I am so ready! This is going to be easy. Three, two, one...

Jen: Wait! What are we supposed to be doing?

Ben: Oh, you don't know? It's a race to the finish through this incredibly tough assault course.

Jen: Oh. OK.

Ben: Three, two, one...

Jen: Wait! Shouldn't we have a referee?

Ben: Fine. REFEREE!

[Enter stage – Referee]

Referee: You both know the rules?

Ben: Yes!

Jen: Kind of.

Referee: Shake hands.

[Ben and Jen Shake hands]

Referee: High five.

[Ben and Jen high five]

Referee: Kiss.

[Ben puckers up]

Jen: NO! What's wrong with you!?

Referee: On your marks, get set... *[Blows whistle]*

[Ben and Jen begin making their way up and over and through the assault course. Immediately, several people make their way on stage and begin to try and stop both Ben and Jen from completing the race. They stand in their way, they squirt them with water pistols. They tell them that they're rubbish and that they should give up. Ben keeps on stopping and getting annoyed, whereas Jen continues with the race, ignoring everyone until she eventually finishes the race. Ben is still at the start]

Discouragers: You're rubbish Ben! You'll never finish. Ben is a loser. Ben is a loser. Ben is a loser. Ben is a loser.

Ben: You know what. I've had it. No one told me this was going to happen. I can't be doing with this. I give up.

[Exit stage – Ben]

Referee: *[Handing Jen a trophy]* Congratulations to... Jen, the winner! Jen, is there anything you'd like to say?

Jen: I'd just like to thank my Mum and my Dad, and all the other people who made this possible. You know, there's a saying that goes something like...

Referee: *[Interrupting]* OK. Thank you. That's all we have time for. Goodbye! *[Exit stage – Referee and Discouragers]*

Jen: Where's Ben? Ben! *[Enter stage – Ben]*

Ben: What!?

Jen: What happened?

Ben: Nothing.

Jen: Did all of those people calling you a loser make you give up?

Ben: No... Maybe... Yes.

Jen: You're not a loser, Ben. Come on. Let's get a cup of tea.

Ben: OK.

Jen: Have you seen my trophy!? Look how cool it is. This is what you could've won!

Ben: That is NOT helpful, Jen.

Jen: Sorry, Ben.

[Exit stage – Ben and Jen]

ACT ○ PUPPETS

HOW CAN I KEEP MY EYES FIXED ON JESUS?

[Enter – Jack and Jill. Jack is intently looking up at the ceiling]

Jill: Hello everyone. I'm Jill, and this here is my friend, Jack… Jack, are you going to say anything?

Jack: Anything.

Jill: No, not the word, 'anything'. Are you going to say hello to the people? *[Pause]* Actually, forget it! What are you doing?

Jack: Jill, I am so pleased you asked. Perhaps you'd like to join me and I'll explain.

Jill: You want me to look up at the ceiling, too?

Jack: Yes.

Jill: OK. Bear with us everyone. I'm sure there'll be an extremely good explanation coming up soon.

[Jill does as Jack requests and looks up]

Jack: You see, Jill, I heard someone mention earlier that we should be keeping our eyes fixed on Jesus. I've been looking for Jesus and can't find Him, but my best guess is that He is somewhere… up there. So I'm going to keep my eyes fixed up there… on Jesus.

Jill: Oh dear. I'm sorry everyone. Jack, stop looking up please.

Jack: No can do. Sorry.

Jill: Can you look at me please?

Jack: I would, but my eyes are fixed on Jesus.

Jill: Hmm… You could at least blink. Your eyes will get sore.

Jack: OK…

[Jack tries to blink. He then stops looking up and stares at the audience]

Jack: Jill!

Jill: Yes, Jack?

Jack: Jill… I can't blink! My eyes won't close! They're stuck! ARRRRRR! Help me! Fetch a doctor, or an optician… or an eye pad.

Jill: Calm down, Jack. You don't have eye lids, remember? You're a puppet.

Jack: Oh… But I want to be a real boy.

Jill: Then you must first prove yourself to be brave and truthful and selfless… then you shall become a real boy… Hmm, I think we're crossing stories here. How are your eyes, Jack?

Jack: They're fine. I'm just a bit annoyed at you for stopping me keeping my eyes fixed on Jesus.

Jill: Jack, I think you've misunderstood what "keeping your eyes fixed on Jesus" actually means.

Jack: I have?

Jill: Yes. You see, "keeping your eyes fixed on Jesus" does not mean that you have to keep looking at wherever Jesus is, or keep looking at a picture of Jesus; and before you go there, nor does it mean taking your eyes out and sticking them onto Jesus' clothes.

Jack: That's gross, Jill. What's wrong with you?

Jill: Fixing your eyes on Jesus is actually about following Jesus.

Jack: Then I need to follow Him? Fine. Where is He? How close behind Him do I need to stay? Should I keep a distance of seventy-five cubits?

Jill: No! Hmmm, this is tricky. To keep your eyes fixed on Jesus is like keeping your mind fixed on Jesus. It means to be thinking, what would Jesus do in this situation, or, what does Jesus want me to do, or, where does He want me to go, how does He want me to act. That kind of thing.

Jack: Oh, so to copy Jesus?

Jill: Yes, I guess so. But also praying and asking Him what He wants you to do.

Jack: Phew. I seriously thought I was going to have to look up for the rest of my life. It was going to be tricky walking home later; and eating my dinner; and going to the toilet.

Jill: That's enough, Jack. We should probably go now.

Jack: OK. Bye everyone.

Jill: Bye!

[Exit – Jack and Jill]

SONG INFORMATION FOR SECTIONS 1-3

Everybody's Welcome Nigel Hemming • © 2008 Vineyard Songs (UK/Eire) (Adm. Song Solutions www.songsolutions.org) CCLI# 5338281

1 PERSEVERANCE

Awesome Is The Lord Most High Cary Pierce / Chris Tomlin / Jesse Reeves / Jon Abel • © 2006 45 Degrees Music/Bridge Building Music, Inc/ Popular Purple Media (Small Stone Media / Song Solutions www.songsolutions.org): sixsteps Music / Vamos Publishing / worshiptogether.com songs (Adm. by CapitolCMGPublishing.com excl. UK & Europe, adm. by Integrity Music, part of the David C Cook family, songs@integritymusic.com) CCLI# 4674159

Strong And Brave Steve Squires • © Song Solutions www.songsolutions.org CCLI# 6494069

To God Be The Glory Words: Fanny Crosby / William Goward Doane / Music Arr: Damian Herbert • © Words: Public Domain / Music: 2014 Song Solutions www.songsolutions.org CCLI# 7035105

Blessed Be Your Name Beth and Matt Redman • © 2002 Thankyou Music (Adm. by CapitolCMGPublishing.com excl. UK & Europe, adm. by Integrity Music, part of the David C Cook family, songs@integritymusic.com) CCLI# 3798438

Be Thou My Vision Dallan Forgaill / Eleanor Henrietta Hull / Mary Elizabeth Byrne • Public Domain CCLI# 7020083

You Never Let Go Beth and Matt Redman • © 2007 Thankyou Music (Adm. by CapitolCMGPublishing.com excl. UK & Europe, adm. by Integrity Music, part of the David C Cook family, songs@integritymusic.com) CCLI# 4674166

I Have Decided To Follow Jesus Unknown • Public Domain CCLI# 7017581

Be The Centre Michael Frye • © 1999 Vineyard Songs (UK/Eire) (Adm. Song Solutions www.songsolutions.org) CCLI# 2650429

God Is Our Strength And Refuge Richard Bewes • © 1982 The Jubilate Group (Admin by The Jubilate Group) CCLI# 2607575

Hosanna (Praise Is Rising) Brenton Brown / Paul Baloche • © 2005, 2006 Integrity's Hosanna! Music & Thankyou Music (Adm. by CapitolCMGPublishing.com excl. UK & Europe, adm. by Integrity Music, part of the David C Cook family, songs@integritymusic.com) CCLI# 4662491

Shout To The Lord (My Jesus, My Saviour) Darlene Zschech • ©1993 Wondrous Worship (Adm. Song Solutions www.songsolutions.org) CCLI# 1406918

Everlasting God (Strength Will Rise) Brenton Brown / Ken Riley • © 2005 Thankyou Music (Adm. by CapitolCMGPublishing.com excl. UK & Europe, adm. by Integrity Music, part of the David C Cook family, songs@integritymusic.com) CCLI# 4556538

2 GOD IS LOVE

Forever (Give Thanks To The Lord) Chris Tomlin • © 2001 sixsteps Music/worshiptogether.com songs (Adm. by CapitolCMGPublishing.com excl. UK & Europe, adm. by Integrity Music, part of the David C Cook family, songs@integritymusic.com) CCLI# 3148428

Walk With You Damian Herbert / Steve Squires • © Song Solutions www.songsolutions.org CCLI# 6493950

Love The Lord Your God Lincoln Brewster • © 2005 Integrity's Praise! Music (Adm. by CapitolCMGPublishing.com excl. UK & Europe, adm. by Integrity Music, part of the David C Cook family, songs@integritymusic.com) CCLI# 4572938

With My Whole Heart Graham Kendrick • © 1981 Thankyou Music (Adm. by CapitolCMGPublishing.com excl. UK & Europe, adm. by Integrity Music, part of the David C Cook family, songs@integritymusic.com) CCLI# 223020

I Will Sing Your Praises (Father God I Wonder) Ian Smale (Ishmael) • © 1984 Thankyou Music (Adm. by CapitolCMGPublishing.com excl. UK & Europe, adm. by Integrity Music, part of the David C Cook family, songs@integritymusic.com) CCLI# 58202

Here Is Love William Rees, William Williams • Public Domain CCLI# 2682882

How Deep The Father's Love Stuart Townend • © 1995 Thankyou Music (Adm. by CapitolCMGPublishing.com excl. UK & Europe, adm. by Integrity Music, part of the David C Cook family, songs@integritymusic.com) CCLI# 1558110

God's Love Is So Wonderful Traditional • Public Domain

I Stand Amazed (My Saviour's Love) Charles H Gabriel • Public Domain CCLI# 25297

Here I Am To Worship (Light Of The World) Tim Hughes • © 2000 Thankyou Music (Adm. by CapitolCMGPublishing.com excl. UK & Europe, adm. by Integrity Music, part of the David C Cook family, songs@integritymusic.com) CCLI# 3266032

Amazing Love (My Lord, What Love Is This) Graham Kendrick • © 1989 Make Way Music www.grahamkendrick.co.uk CCLI# 192553

One Thing Remains Brian Johnson / Christa Black Gifford / Jeremy Riddle • © 2010 Bethel Music Publishing / Christa Joy Music Publishing / Mercy/Vineyard Publishing (Adm. by Vineyard Music USA) (Adm. Song Solutions www.songsolutions.org) CCLI# 5508444

I Could Sing Of Your Love Forever Martin Smith • © 1994 Curious? Music UK (Adm. by CapitolCMGPublishing.com excl. UK & Europe, adm. by Integrity Music, part of the David C Cook family, songs@integritymusic.com) CCLI# 1043199

Such Love Graham Kendrick • © 1988 Make Way Music www.grahamkendrick.co.uk CCLI# 30536

Hallelujah (Your Love Is Amazing) Brenton Brown / Brian Doerksen • © 2000 Vineyard Songs (UK/Eire) (Adm. Song Solutions www.songsolutions.org) CCLI# 3091812

3 GOD PROTECTS

10,000 Reasons (Bless The Lord) Jonas Myrin / Matt Redman • © 2011 Said And Done Music/sixsteps Music/worshiptogether. com songs/Thankyou Music (Adm. by CapitolCMGPublishing.com excl. UK & Europe, adm. by Integrity Music, part of the David C Cook family, songs@integritymusic.com): SHOUT! Music Publishing (Admin. By HMRT Limited CCLI# 6016351

Mighty To Save (Everyone Needs Compassion) Ben Fielding / Reuben Morgan • © 2006 Hillsong Music Publishing (APRA) All rights reserved. International copyright secured CCLI# 4591782

Whole World In His Hands Arr: Damian Herbert • © 2008 Song Solutions www.songsolutions.org CCLI# 5345834

Faithful One Brian Doerksen • © 1989 Mercy/ Vineyard Publishing / Vineyard Songs Canada (Admin by Vineyard Music USA) (Adm. Song Solutions www.songsolutions.org) CCLI# 465840

Lord For The Years (Lord Of The Years) Timothy Dudley-Smith • © 1976 Timothy Dudley-Smith (Admin. By Oxford University Press) CCLI# 3274952

Love Came Down (I've Found A Love) Ben Cantelon • © 2006 Thankyou Music (Adm. by CapitolCMGPublishing.com excl. UK & Europe, adm. by Integrity Music, part of the David C Cook family, songs@integritymusic.com) CCLI# 4943316

My Lighthouse Rend Collective • © 2013 Thankyou Music (Adm. by CapitolCMGPublishing.com excl. UK & Europe, adm. by Integrity Music, part of the David C Cook family, songs@integritymusic.com) CCLI# 7002032

Oceans (Where Feet May Fail) Joel Houston / Matt Crocker / Salomon Ligthelm • © 2012 Hillsong Music Publishing (APRA) All rights reserved. International copyright secured CCLI# 6428767

Whom Shall I Fear (God Of Angel Armies) Chris Tomlin / Ed Cash / Scott Cash • © 2012 S.D.G. Publishing/Sixsteps Songs/Worship Together Music (Adm. by CapitolCMGPublishing.com excl. UK & Europe, adm. by Integrity Music, part of the David C Cook family, songs@integritymusic. com): Alletrop Music / McTyeire Music (Adm. Song Solutions www.songsolutions.org) CCLI# 6440288

GOD IS LOVE

2

THEME

The main theme
for this service is **God is love.**

Love is a word that is full of so much variety and meaning.
It's good to be reminded of what true love really is, and
God's love for us is the truest form.

STORY

God made the world
and everything in it.

God made the world and everything in it. Then He made people – and
according to the text in Genesis, that creation process was a bit different
from the rest of creation. God spoke, and there was light, land, sky, trees, the
sun, the moon, stars and animals. When it came to making people, He got
messy. He got some of His newly created mud and formed it into a man, and
He breathed into the man the breath of life – His breath.

We are lovingly created by a God who is by nature, love.

IDEAS

This service would fit nicely into the
second week of February if you
fancy a **Valentine's Day Special.**

You could even theme the whole church and have heart biscuits
or Love Heart sweets around as little treats!

ORDER OF SERVICE

3 MINS · **INTRODUCTION / WELCOME**

3 MINS · **SING** *Everybody's Welcome*

2 MINS · **PRAY** Psalm 136: *His love goes on forever*

3 MINS

SING *Forever (Give Thanks To The Lord)*

MOVE Sign language

THINK Love quotes

3 MINS · **CREATE** Make people

8 MINS · **ACT** *Adam and Eve*

SCRIPT *see page 37*

2 MINS · **TELL 1** God created out of love

SCRIPT *see page 32*

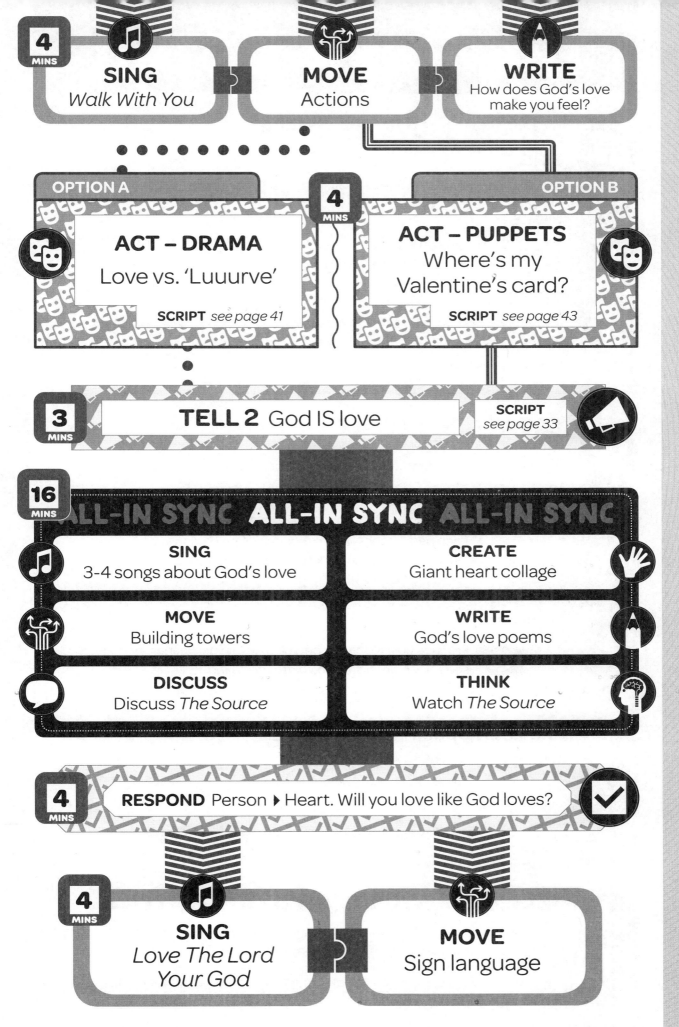

4 MINS

SING *Walk With You*

MOVE Actions

WRITE How does God's love make you feel?

OPTION A

4 MINS

OPTION B

ACT – DRAMA Love vs. 'Luuurve'

SCRIPT *see page 41*

ACT – PUPPETS Where's my Valentine's card?

SCRIPT *see page 43*

3 MINS

TELL 2 God IS love

SCRIPT *see page 33*

16 MINS

ALL-IN SYNC ALL-IN SYNC ALL-IN SYNC

SING 3-4 songs about God's love

CREATE Giant heart collage

MOVE Building towers

WRITE God's love poems

DISCUSS Discuss *The Source*

THINK Watch *The Source*

4 MINS

RESPOND Person ▸ Heart. Will you love like God loves?

4 MINS

SING *Love The Lord Your God*

MOVE Sign language

THE FINER DETAIL

SING ▸ MOVE ▸ THINK

SING

Lead the congregation in *Forever (Give Thanks To The Lord)***.

MOVE

 Sign language on the pre-chorus and chorus –
see *www.bigministries.co.uk/theallinthing*.

THINK

Invite those who would like to, to find some quotes about love – from memory, Bible verses or quotes online. Write these up on a board, or send them to the Tech Team to display on the screen, or even text them to someone to write up elsewhere.

CREATE ◉ PEOPLE

The Most-Prep Option Personal people

You need: Cut out people templates – one per person
Felt tip pens

Each person should turn their template person
into something that looks a bit like them!

The Only-Got-to-Practice-Prep Option Pipe cleaner people

You need: Pipe cleaners – one per person

 Practice how to make a person from a pipe cleaner –
see *www.bigministries.co.uk/theallinthing*.

Lead everyone in creating their person.

The Messy Option Play-dough people

You need: Lots of play-dough
Paper plates – one per person
Tools for shaping play-dough (optional)

Allow everyone the time to create a person from their play-dough.

TELL 1 ◉ GOD CREATED OUT OF LOVE

God made everything. The story we just heard skipped over it, but He did. He started with nothing, He spoke, and everything came into being.

Then He got to the people... and all of a sudden He changed His technique.

God handcrafted a man, and He breathed His breath into him to make him come to life. We were lovingly created by a God of love. He formed us with care to be in relationship with Him.

Wowsers! Think about how special that makes us. The God who can do ANYTHING formed humans out of mud and personally filled our lungs with His breath. Amazing!

But you heard the end of the story too; it didn't end quite as beautifully. Adam and Eve went away from God's plan, and damaged that beautiful relationship.

So God, heart-broken and desperate to fix it, had to do something drastic – and so He "stepped into the world that He had made" (do this with the signs)… (Talk through some of the next song, and then lead people in it.)

SING ▶ MOVE ▶ WRITE

SING

Walk With You* – this song is on *The All-In Thing Songs* CD.

MOVE

▶ Sign language – see *www.bigministries.co.uk/theallinthing*.

We recommend using the full track for this song, as the emphasis will be on moving, telling the story and using the sign language to worship.

WRITE

How does God's love make you feel?

TELL 2 ⊙ GOD IS LOVE

God's love is so much more than romantic love. The love that we experience on Valentine's Day is all about emotion and feeling good.

The love that God has for us is strong, it is protective, it is faithful, it is unconditional and sometimes it is painful.

God shows His love for us in ways that are so real. God doesn't send us Valentine's cards or flowers. God doesn't engrave our initials in a heart on a tree (although He could if He wanted to!).

God ultimately showed His love for us by sending Jesus into the world to fix the mess we made.

But God does even more than show us love. He IS love. There is nothing about Him that isn't love.

God IS love.

THE FINER DETAIL **GOD IS LOVE**

SING

Sing a few songs about God's love.

With My Whole Heart
Graham Kendrick

Father God I Wonder
Ian Smale (Ishmael)

Here Is Love William Rees,
William Williams, Robery Lowry

How Deep The Father's Love
Stuart Townend

God's Love Is So Wonderful
Traditional

I Stand Amazed In The Presence
Charles H. Gabriel

*Here I Am To Worship (Light Of
The World)* Tim Hughes

*My Lord, What Love Is This
(Amazing Love)* Graham Kendrick

One Thing Remains Brian Johnson,
Christa Black-Gifford, Jeremy Riddle

I Could Sing Of Your Love Forever
Martin Smith

Such Love
Graham Kendrick

Hallelujah (Your Love Is Amazing)
Brenton Brown, Brian Doerksen

Copyright details for these songs can be found on page 28.

CREATE • Collage Heart

Provide a giant heart outline, glue, scissors and lots of magazines, tissue paper, glitter, glue, sequins, bits of wool and basically anything that can be stuck on!

During the activity, or when the drawing is finished, talk about:

How does God show us that He is love?

How can we show other people the same love that God shows us?

MOVE • Building Towers

Provide lots of building materials:
Jenga bricks / wooden blocks / Lego / Duplo / even cardboard boxes.

Instruct people to build the tallest, strongest tower they can.

Talk about:

Ephesians 3:17-18 *(The Message)*

And I ask Him that with both feet planted firmly on love, you'll be able to take in with all followers of Jesus the extravagant dimensions of Christ's love. Reach out and experience the breadth! Test its length! Plumb the depths! Rise to the heights! Live full lives, full in the fullness of God.

Is there anything stronger than God's love?

Not even death?

WRITE

Make sure you have some nice writing paper, nice pens and Bibles available.

"Write a love poem as if God had written it to you."

DISCUSS

Someone leading the discussion is ideal.

▶ Watch *The Source* (Search *Ethos – The Source* on YouTube).

Discuss:

"Love is just words until action prevails." Is this true?

"His message is love and with this love He frees us."
What does this love free us from?

How can we live like people free in God's love?

Who do we need to love (like The Source *loves us) more?*

THINK

Make available: Bibles, cushions, ear defenders, paper, pens and even mp3 players with headphones.

▶ Watch *The Source* (Search *Ethos – The Source* on YouTube).

Think about:

"Love is just words until action prevails." Is this true?

"His message is love and with this love He frees us."
What does this love free us from?

How can we live like people free in God's love?

Who do we need to love (like The Source *loves us) more?*

RESPOND

Do we live like people who have a secure knowledge of God's unconditional and unending love for us? Are we ready to commit to loving people as God loves us?

If so, you could invite people to turn their person into a heart to show they are ready to be a person of love.

You could say this closing prayer together. Teach the congregation the line they say in response before beginning the prayer. The response line is in **bold.**

GOD IS LOVE THE FINER DETAIL

God of love
We confess we are sometimes impatient, and often unkind.
We are quick to envy and find subtle ways to boast.
There are times when we are rude, and lift ourselves up as we put others down.
Loving God, teach us to love like you.

God of love
We confess that we are quickly angered.
We are quick to record how often we've been wronged.
There are times when we celebrate the misfortunes of others.
Loving God, teach us to love like you.

God of love
We confess that we put ourselves first.
We're reluctant to give, we are slow to sacrifice.
There are times when we hesitate to protect.
Loving God, teach us to love like you.

When we are tempted to judge, to assume the worst...
May love remind us to trust.
When we are tempted to despair, to assume all is lost...
May love remind us to hope.
When we are tempted to give up, to assume it will never happen...
May love remind us to persevere.
Loving God, teach us to love like you.
Amen.

SING MOVE

SING

Love The Lord Your God* – this song is on *The All-In Thing Songs* CD.

MOVE

▶ Sign language – see *www.bigministries.co.uk/theallinthing*.

There's potential to add new verses to this song based on where you feel the service needs to focus at the end, e.g. "We will love you, Lord" or "We will love your world".

PRAY

It's not on the order of service, but do close the service with prayer!

ACT ● STORY
ADAM AND EVE ● GENESIS 2: 7-3

Characters:
- ◉ Narrator 1
- ◉ Narrator 2
- ◉ Adam
- ◉ Eve
- ◉ Voice of God
- ◉ Serpent

You will need:
- ◉ Toy animals
- ◉ Tree of the Knowledge of Good and Evil
- ◉ Fruit
- ◉ Two jackets – leather if possible
- ◉ Spade and watering can
- ◉ Fig leaf

Teach the audience these **trigger words** *before reading the story:*

Man	*A* **manly cheer** *from the men.*
Woman	*A* **lady-like "woop"** *from the women.*
Animals	*Choose an animal and* **make the noise.**
Trees	*Make yourself* **look like a tree and say "I'm a tree!".**

Narrator 1: It was the sixth day of the creation of the world. God had already placed so much colour and wonder and beauty onto the Earth.

Narrator 2: The sky, sea, sun, moon, stars, plants, trees, birds, fish and **animals**.

Narrator 1: But God had not quite finished. For there was more to be made.

Narrator 2: God took some dirt from the earth and then began to mould and sculpt and perfect His creation – **Man**.

Narrator 1: God then breathed the breath of life into the nostrils of the **man** and the **man** became a living being!

[There is no sign of Adam]

Narrator 1: I said... "and the **man** became a living being."... Adam! Where are you!?

[Adam doesn't yet enter stage but shouts from off stage]

Adam: I'm back here... I was just thinking.

Narrator 2: What were you thinking?

Adam: Well... It's a bit embarrassing but, am I supposed to be naked?

Narrator 2: Erm, yes... but I think in this situation it's probably best that you just keep your clothes on.

> You could place images of each part of creation on a screen as they are read aloud by the narrator.

Adam: Phew... OK. *[Enter stage – Adam]* Ta-da! Here I am.

Narrator 1: Now, God had planted a garden in a place called Eden. This is where He placed Adam.

[Enter stage – the Tree of the Knowledge of Good and Evil and a whole load of toy animals]

Narrator 2: Adam was to look after and take care of the garden and everything in it, such as the **trees** and the **animals**.

[Adam is handed a spade and a watering can]

Adam: Wow! This is incredible. Look at all of these **animals**. I'm going to name them... This one can be called... *[picking up a couple of animals]* a sausage! And this other one... a pong-stencher.

Narrator 1: I think we may need to work on some of the names.

Narrator 2: Next, God took a rib out of Adam and made a partner for him, as He didn't think that Adam should be alone.

Adam: A rib!? From my body? That sounds painful. I don't think I'm happy with this.

Narrator 1: God put Adam into a deep sleep *[Adam collapses on the floor]*, removed one of his ribs...

Adam: *[Talking in his sleep]* Ooh, that tickles.

Narrator 2: ... and then sealed up the wound.

Narrator 1: From the rib, a **woman** was created to keep Adam company.

[Enter stage – Eve]

Eve: Hey everyone!

[Adam wakes up and looks at the woman]

Narrator 2: Adam then said,

Adam: Hey there. *[Placing hand on the woman's shoulder]* You are bone of my bones, and flesh of my flesh. You shall be called, 'Foxy'.

Narrator 1: No, Adam.

Adam: You shall be called, 'Chick'.

Narrators 1 and 2: No!

Adam: 'Babe'?

Narrators 1 and 2: No!

Adam: 'Bird'?

Narrators 1 and 2: No!

Adam: 'Hotty'?

Narrators 1 and 2: No!

Adam: 'Sugar plum'?

Narrators 1 and 2: No!

Narrator 2: Enough!... She shall be called, **'Woman'**, because she was taken out of **man**.

If you're feeling brave, you could have a couple of people dressed as animals to run and skip across stage (for comedy value) and then exit.

You could also have someone dress up as the Tree of the Knowledge of Good and Evil.

Adam: Fine. I'll name this **'Woman'**, Eve.

Narrator 1: So, Adam, the **man**, and Eve, the **woman**, enjoyed each other's company and looked after the garden together.

Narrator 2: Until, one day, a crafty serpent made its way over to the **woman** and said to her,

[Enter stage – Serpent]

Serpent: Eve…

Narrator 1: And Eve said…

Eve: Ahhh! A talking snake! I mean, yes?

Serpent: Did God really say that you can't eat from the **trees** in the garden?

Eve: No. Not at all. Just one. The one in the middle. Apparently, if we eat from it or even touch it, then we'll die.

Serpent: Ha. Is that what He said? That is so funny. Of course you won't die. The fruit on it is part of your five-a-day. God only said that because He knows that when you eat from it, you'll become like Him, knowing both good and evil and everything in between. Oh dear. I've gone and said too much haven't I? I'd best be going.

Eve: Hmmm… the fruit on the **tree** does look good. Maybe I should… Yep. I'm eating it.

Narrator 1: So, Eve took the fruit and ate it.

Narrator 2: Then she handed the fruit to Adam, who also ate it.

Narrator 1: Immediately something changed in them and they became ashamed that they were naked… *[Adam and Eve look at each other, confused because they actually have clothes on]* Just pretend you're naked, OK?

Eve: Fine. Arrrrghh! We're naked!

Adam: Yeah we are *[wink]*… I mean… Oh no, we're naked!

Eve: Quick, cover yourself with this fig leaf. *[Handing Adam a small fig leaf]*

Adam: Seriously? Can you not find anything bigger?

Narrator 2: Adam and Eve then heard God. He was walking through the garden, through the **trees**, amongst the **animals**, and He called out to them, but they hid.

Eve: Quick! Over here! God will never see us if we hide down here.

[Eve grabs Adam's hand and pulls him down, crouching on the floor]

Adam: If only we had a lead roof. God can't see through lead.

Eve: You are full of such rubbish.

God: Where are you?

[Adam realises that it's no good hiding and stands up]

Adam: *[Sigh]* I'm here. So's Eve. We hid from you because we were naked.

God: Who told you that you were naked? Did you eat from the one **tree** that I told you not to eat from?

Adam and Eve: *[Sigh]* Yes.

Adam and Eve could use spades and watering cans etc as they look after the Garden of Eden.

Narrator 1: So, God made the **man** and the **woman** some leather clothing and dressed them.

[Enter stage – a couple of stage hands with leather jackets for Adam and Eve]

Adam: I told you that fig leaf was ridiculous! I look so cool in this jacket.

Narrator 2: Then, God punished both of them and kicked them out of the garden.

[Exit stage – Adam and Eve with heads hung low]

Narrator 1: So, Adam and Eve lived together and looked after one another... and had babies and stuff.

Narrator 2: But never again did they enter the Garden of Eden.

Narrator 1: And never again were things perfect.

Narrator 2: The end... of the beginning.

ACT ○ DRAMA

LOVE VS. 'LUUURVE'

You will need:
- A table
- A few homemade Valentine's Day cards
- A tube of *Swizzels Matlow* Love Hearts

[Enter stage – Ben, who begins setting up Valentine's Day cards on table]

Ben: Ladies and gentlemen, roll up, roll up! If you have not yet given your special someone a Valentine's Day card then you are indeed the lucky ones here among us today. For I, Ben, CEO of GroovyChicken.com – *[aside]* website under construction – have revolutionised Valentine's Day cards.

[Enter stage – Jen]

Jen: Erm, Ben?

Ben: In fact, not only have I revolutionised Valentine's Day cards but I have revolutionised love. No longer must we tolerate all this 'luuurve' nonsense during this Valentine's season but...

Jen: *[Interrupting]* Ben? What are you doing?

Ben: *[To Jen]* Jen, please, I am in the middle of my sales pitch. *[To congregation]* As I was saying, no longer must we tolerate...

Jen: *[Interrupting]* Ben, what on earth are you doing? Are you selling Valentine's Day cards in a church service?

Ben: *[To Jen]* Well, Jen, I like to think of it more like I'm revolutionising love but if it helps you to understand it then yes, I suppose I am selling Valentine's Day cards in a church service. *[To congregation]* Ahem, no longer must we tolerate...

Jen: *[Interrupting]* Ben! Ben! Just stop a second. Did you happen to make these yourself?

Ben: Why, yes. Yes I did.

Jen: What makes you think that anyone here wants to buy a handmade Valentine's Day card?

Ben: Because, Jen, everyone here is fed up with all this Valentine's 'luuurve' nonsense. 'Luuurve' is just about gooey feelings, but love, love is different. Love is deeper than that. Love is better than 'luuurve' and people want to send cards that say how much their loved ones really mean to them. My exclusive cards make their dreams a reality.

Jen: Let me see one of those... *[Reading front]* "My Valentine, I want to spend most of forever with you". Most of? Why only most of?

Ben: Well, for one, most toilet trips should remain a one-player game.

Jen: OK, let's move on quickly. What about this card? *[Reading the front of another card]* "I love you just the way you are." Aah, that's actually quite nice. What does the inside say? *[Reading inside]* "But I would love you a little bit more if your bottom was a little bit less..." Ben, you can't say that, it's mean!

Ben: Yes I can, and no it's not mean, it's love. It's like I told you before: I'm revolutionising love.

Jen: Right, and you think that you can revolutionise love just by making some slightly offensive cards?

Ben: No Jen, that would be ridiculous... I also have a line of custom-made Love Heart sweets. *[Revealing a tube of Love Hearts and giving Jen a sweet]* Whoever made Love Hearts left the backs blank for your own message. I have taken the liberty of filling them in. In so doing, I have changed gooey messages of 'luuurve' into meaningful messages of love.

Jen: *[Reading]* "You're my number one..." *[turning sweet over]* "... not including food or XBox." Ben, this is just silly.

Ben: No, Jen. All this 'luuurve' stuff is silly. Love is not silly. Love is better than 'luuurve'.

Jen: Yes, you already said that, but love isn't just saying the same things and adding some sort of small print to point out what you don't like.

Ben: It's not?

Jen: No, it's not. Real love doesn't have small print; it doesn't have conditions and it's not about how you're feeling. Real love is kind and...

Ben: Oh, OK. So, I'm not revolutionising love then?

Jen: No, I'm not sure you are.

Ben: Well, that's disappointing. Do you want to buy a card anyway?

Jen: No.

Ben: Please, I spent ages on them. I've invested capital!

Jen: No.

Ben: Fine. Would you like a customised Love Heart instead?

Jen: Yes, I will take one of those. *[Eating a Love Heart]* Urgh, is that Biro I can taste?

Ben: No... Maybe.

[Exit stage – Ben and Jen]

ACT ● PUPPETS

WHERE'S MY VALENTINE'S CARD?

Jill: Happy Valentine's Day, Jack! How many cards did you get?

Jack: Erm... Seven hundred aaaand... twenty... three.

Jill: Jack, you don't even know that many people. How many did you really get?

Jack: Just one... from my Mum.

Jill: Oh, that's nice, Jack... *[Pause]* ... Are you going to ask me how many I got?

Jack: How many did you get?

Jill: I don't know, let me just count them.

[Jill disappears behind puppet screen and begins counting]

Jill: One... two... three... four... five... six... seven... eight...

Jack: Is this going to take long?

Jill: Yes, probably... nine... ten... eleven... twelve... thirteen...

Jack: OK, Jill! I get it. You've got loads of Valentine's Day cards. Well done, you!

[Jill comes back]

Jill: Are you OK, Jack? You seem a little bit – now how do I put this delicately? – You seem a little bit stroppy. A bit of a stroppy pants. Am I right? Are you being a big stroppy pants?

Jack: I am NOT being a big stroppy pants.

Jill: You are a being a bit of a big stroppy pants.

Jack: I am not!

Jill: Is it because I got more Valentine's Day cards than you?

Jack: No!

Jill: Is it because... Hmmm... Nope, I can't think of anything else. Is it because I got more Valentine's Day cards than you?

Jack: No, Jill. It's not that, OK!

Jill: Fine. What is it then?

Jack: Well... I was expecting a Valentine's Day card from someone else.

Jill: Oh, Jack... I see what's going on. Is it because you're in love with me and I didn't give you a Valentine's Day card?

Jack: What!? No! Gross.

Jill: Easy, Jack. A girl's got feelings you know.

Jack: Where was my Valentine's Day card from God?

Jill: From God?

Jack: What are you, a parrot? Yes, from God.

Jill: *[Confused pause]* From God?

Jack: God is supposed to love me. It turns out that the only person who loves me is my Mum, as she's the only one who got me a card. I expected more from God. I thought He loved me.

Jill: Of course He loves you, Jack.

Jack: Well, the lack of a card says otherwise.

Jill: Well, the fact that He sent Jesus to Earth for you says that He does. What do you think about that, huh?! Jill, one; Jack, nil.

Jack: Well... erm... Yes, I see your point... But I wanted a card.

Jill: I don't think God needs to send you a card to show you that He loves you, Jack. He shows you in much better ways. I guess we're sometimes just not as good at showing love... and so... that's why we have cards... maybe?

Jack: Oh... I see. So cards aren't that important.

Jill: Well, I wouldn't go that far. Did you see how many I got?

Jack: Cards aren't important and God does love me! Phew. This day just got a lot better! Thanks, Jill.

Jill: Back to my Valentine's Day cards though, Jack. I did get quite a lot.

Jack: Jill, God loves me. I'm going to go away and think of more things that God has done to show me that He loves me. Bye everyone!

[Exit – Jack]

Jill: Great idea, Jack, but... my cards. I have lots of cards... Oh, I give up. Happy Valentine's everyone. See you soon.

[Exit – Jill]

GOD PROTECTS

3

THEME

The main theme for this service is **God protects.**

The whole service is also based around the theme of **Mothering Sunday** (we know that a lot of churches do a special service on Mothering Sunday, so we thought we'd try to help!). God's protection for us as His children could be likened to the protecting love of a mother for her children.

STORY

Jochebed – Moses' mother – **was an amazing woman**, and a very brave one at that!

She gave birth to a son at just the wrong time... Just the time that the not-so-friendly Pharaoh decided the Hebrews were taking over, so he needed to kill all the baby boys. Jochebed hid Moses for three months (which is a mighty feat in itself – newborns are loud!) and then she risked his, her own and her daughter's life by floating him on the river! It is a strange story to demonstrate a mother's protection – but it does in a rather interesting and dramatic way. Jochebed trusted God, she wholeheartedly believed He would let Moses live, and in this story God shows His ultimate plan and protection for Moses and keeps him safe.

IDEAS

It is always a nice idea to **give out flowers** to the mothers in your congregation.

Perhaps, for this service, flowers (or perhaps chocolate) could be distributed to everyone who has a caring and protecting role...

ORDER OF SERVICE

3 MINS — **INTRODUCTION / WELCOME**

3 MINS — **SING** *Everybody's Welcome*

2 MINS — **PRAY** Psalm 95: 1-3, 6-7 *(The Message)*

4 MINS — **SING** *10,000 Reasons (Bless The Lord)* — **THINK** What are mothers like?

4 MINS — **CREATE** Baskets

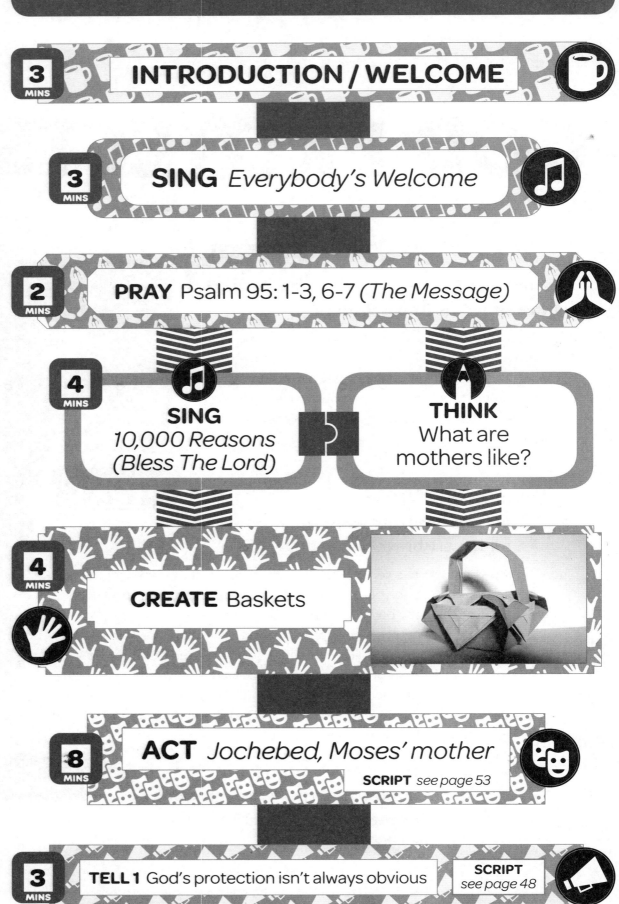

8 MINS — **ACT** *Jochebed, Moses' mother*
SCRIPT *see page 53*

3 MINS — **TELL 1** God's protection isn't always obvious — **SCRIPT** *see page 48*

4 MINS

SING *Mighty To Save*
(Everyone Needs Compassion)

MOVE
Actions

OPTION A

4 MINS

ACT – DRAMA

Mummy's Boy

SCRIPT *see page 57*

OPTION B

ACT – PUPPETS
God can't be like a
mother – He's a man!

SCRIPT *see page 59*

3 MINS

TELL 2 God will always protect us

SCRIPT
see page 49

15 MINS

ALL-IN SYNC **ALL-IN SYNC** ALL-IN SYNC

SING 3-4 songs
about God's protection

CREATE
Build a wall

MOVE
Protect it!

WRITE
A letter to a protector

DISCUSS
How does God protect?

THINK
How does God protect?

2 MINS

RESPOND Give the basket... How can we protect others?

4 MINS

SING
*Whole World In
His Hands*

MOVE
Actions

THINK
Pray for
the world

THE FINER DETAIL

* Copyright details for songs can be found on page 28.

SING THINK

SING

Lead the congregation in *10,000 Reasons (Bless The Lord)***.**

THINK

Invite those who'd like to, to think about what mothers are like.

Provide post-it notes and pens for people to write or draw their ideas and stick them around the church.

CREATE ⊙ BASKETS

The Tricky Option Origami basket

You need: Squares of paper – one per person

 Practice how to make an origami basket - see *www.bigministries.co.uk/theallinthing*.

It's quite tricky, so only embark on this if you're feeling brave!

Lead everyone in creating their basket.

The Medium Option Origami cup

You need: Squares of paper – one per person.

Practice how to make an origami cup - see *www.bigministries.co.uk/theallinthing*.

Lead everyone in creating their cup as a substitute basket!

The Easy, No-Practice-Required Option Foil baskets

You need: Large pieces of foil – one per person
Halved pipe-cleaners – one per person

Lead everyone in scrunching their foil into a basket shape, and attaching (by pushing it through the foil) the pipe-cleaner as a handle.

TELL 1 ⦿ GOD'S PROTECTION ISN'T ALWAYS OBVIOUS

Jochebed is an amazing woman. She did everything she could to protect her little boy. She knew if he was found he would be killed and so she kept him hidden. Just to clarify – she kept a newborn baby hidden for three months, an incredible feat in itself, I think! Then, when she couldn't hide him any longer, she made a waterproof basket and let him float away on the river. Now, it's a pretty crazy story, really. Can you imagine the turmoil for Jochebed? She desperately wanted to be with her son. I've no doubt she just wanted to be with him, keep him close and look after him and yet she knew that doing that would risk his life. If Moses had been aware of what was happening, and what his mother was doing, he might not have felt like his mother was protecting him.

Sometimes God's ways just don't make sense... But He sees the bigger picture. God loves us and God protects us, even if at the time we feel like we are all alone (like Moses floating away in that little basket). God is always keeping an eye out (just like Jochebed sent Miriam to watch the basket) and He will protect us no matter what the cost.

Teach the congregation this phrase: **God will always protect us.**

 Teach the congregation some signs for this too.
Learn the signs at *www.bigministries.co.uk/theallinthing*.

SING MOVE

SING

Everyone Needs Compassion*.

MOVE

 Actions on the chorus – see *www.bigministries.co.uk/theallinthing* (these actions were made up by some children we met on a church weekend away!).

TELL 2 ◉ GOD WILL ALWAYS PROTECT US

"God will always protect us."

It's tricky to think of ways to describe God. Describing Him as "like a mother" is actually a pretty good one, and yet it's still completely inadequate.

God is better than the best parent who has ever lived. God is a perfect parent to us.

God will never let us down, God will always be there for us, God will absolutely love us unconditionally. He will always forgive, He will always be strong and He will never leave us.

God's protection for us is indescribable. God is amazing.

Recap the line and signs – **"God will always protect us."**

SING

Sing a few songs about God's protection of us.

Faithful One
Brian Doerksen

Lord For The Years
Timothy Dudley-Smith

I've Found A Love (Love Came Down)
Ben Cantelon

My Lighthouse
Rend Collective

Oceans (Where Feet May Fail)
Matt Crocker, Joel Houston, Salomon Ligthelm

Whom Shall I Fear (God Of Angel Armies) Ed Cash, Scott Cash, Chris Tomlin

You Never Let Go
Beth Redman, Matt Redman

Copyright details for these songs can be found on page 28.

CREATE • Build a wall

Ideally collect a load of boxes over the weeks prior to this service to enable the building of a three-dimensional wall.

Provide paints, pens, tissue paper, marker pens.

Invite people to decorate the boxes to look like bricks.

When they are decorated, ask them to write truths about God on them with marker pens (or stick on paper with these words on).

Build the bricks into a wall – gluing them together if possible – somewhere where everyone can see it.

If you are not able to collect boxes, a two-dimensional wall could easily be constructed with pieces of decorated paper stuck to an existing wall.

MOVE

Super-active Goalkeeping activity

You will need:

- A football goal
- Footballs
- 'Valuable-looking' plastic vases filled with liquid (if outside)

Place the vases inside the back of the goal.

Invite the people in this zone to take it in turns to be the 'protector'. They must do everything they can (even if it's not orthodox football goalkeeping) to protect the vases from the incoming footballs.

Sitting down active Protect The Egg

You will need:

- Newspapers
- Sticky tape
- Eggs
- A-frame ladder

Set the group (or split them if there are lots of people) the challenge of creating a protective transporter for their egg. Something which will protect their egg from breaking when it is dropped from the height of someone standing on the top of the ladder to the floor.

Give them a set time, and then make sure you test them!

During the activity, or when people have completed the game, talk about:

How does it feel to have something valuable which is relying on you to protect it?

What was it like when you allowed the valuable thing to be damaged?

How do you think God feels about protecting us?

WRITE

Make sure you have some nice writing paper, nice pens and Bibles available.

"Write a letter to someone who protects you. (e.g. mother / friend). Think particularly about how their protection of you shows something of God's protection."

DISCUSS

Someone leading the discussion is ideal.

Discuss:

How do we see God's protection every day?

How is God protecting the poor? How can we get involved?

Who are the people in our community who need protection?

What could our church do to protect those in our community who need it?

THINK

Make available: Bibles, cushions, ear defenders, paper, pens, clipboards and even mp3 players with headphones.

Think about:

How do we see God's protection every day?

How is God protecting the poor? How can we get involved?

Who are the people in our community who need protection?

What could our church do to protect those in our community who need it?

RESPOND

Lead people in responding to the message from today.

God protects us, even if we don't always see it or understand His ways. Perhaps say a prayer thanking Him for that.

Ask people to think – how can we show something of His protection to others?

Provide chocolates for everyone to put in their basket.

Invite everyone to think of someone that they want to 'look after'.

Write or draw something nice on the basket, or on paper inside the basket, and add a chocolate.

Invite everyone to give this basket to the person they are going to 'look after' as a sign that they will do just that.

SING MOVE THINK

SING

*Whole World In His Hands** – this song is on *The All-In Thing Songs* CD.

MOVE

▶ Actions – see *www.bigministries.co.uk/theallinthing*.

THINK

Think of countries that need God's protection at the minute. Pray about these now.

PRAY

It's not on the order of service, but do close the service with prayer!

ACT ◉ STORY

JOCHEBED, MOSES' MOTHER ◉ EXODUS 1-2: 1-10

Characters:

◉ Narrator 1
◉ Narrator 2
◉ Pharaoh
◉ Jochebed
◉ Miriam

◉ Pharaoh's Soldier
◉ Princess of Egypt
◉ Baby Moses

You will need:

◉ A basket

---

*Teach the audience these **trigger words** before reading the story:*

Baby

*Either sing the line, **"baby, baby, baby, oooh"** from the song* Baby *by Justin Bieber; or the line, **"rock-a-bye baby, on the treetop"**, from the nursery rhyme.*

River Nile

*Say **"sploosh, splash, splosh!"**. You could divide the audience into three and have one group say **"sploosh"**, the other say **"splash"**, and the other say **"splosh"**, one after the other in that order!*

Narrator 1: After a welcoming invite from Joseph, and after a very 'fruitful' period, the Israelites had settled in Egypt. Joseph was a good guy. I'm sure you all know the story. And if you don't, well, you can find it in the Bible and read it later.

Narrator 2: Now, sometime after Joseph had died, and sometime after the old Egyptian rulers who knew of Joseph had died, a new king was placed on the throne; a new Pharaoh. He was not a good guy.

[Enter stage – Pharaoh]

> For comedy purposes, you could have two servants carrying Pharaoh in on a chair.

Pharaoh: I, Pharaoh – the most handsome, resplendent and significant person to ever grace the Earth – do declare, that all Israelites residing in Egypt shall now be my slaves.

Narrator 1: So, as you can see...

Pharaoh: *[Interrupting]* I'm not finished yet!... Furthermore, I, Pharaoh – the most handsome, resplendent and significant person to ever grace the Earth – do declare that in order to keep control of this Israelite infestation, any newborn boys born into Israelites families will be eradicated from the face of the planet!

Narrator 1: So, as you can see...

Pharaoh: *[Interrupting]* I'm not finished yet!... Furthermore, I, Pharaoh – the most handsome, resplendent and significant person to ever grace the Earth – bid you all a most pleasant week. Goodbye.

[Exit stage – Pharaoh]

Narrator 1: So... As you can see, Pharaoh was one of the most atrocious, evil and obnoxious people to ever grace the Earth.

[Enter stage – Jochebed and Miriam]

Jochebed: Oh Miriam. What are we going to do?

Miriam: Well Mum, I was thinking we could go shopping for some new sandals, then take the new 'no-humped camel', Humphrey, out for a spin. What do you think?

Jochebed: No Miriam! I mean, what are we going to do about this **baby** *[pointing at the baby in her tummy]*? What if it's a boy? If Pharaoh's soldiers find out then they'll...

Miriam: *[Interrupting]* ... I know! I don't know what to do Mum. Let's wait and see what happens. It might be a girl **baby**.

[Exit stage – Jochebed and Miriam]

Narrator 2: And, sometime later, what happened was...

[Enter stage – Jochebed, holding a baby]

Jochebed: ... A boy! It's a beautiful boy!

[Enter stage – Pharaoh's Soldier]

Pharaoh's Soldier: A boy!? Did I hear someone say, 'boy'?

Jochebed: *[Nervous]* Haha... erm... I mean... It's a girl! A beautiful girl...

Pharaoh's Soldier: Hmmm... What was that first thing you said?

Jochebed: What first thing I said?

Pharaoh's Soldier: Hmmm... I've got my eye on you.

[Exit stage – Pharaoh's Soldier]

Jochebed: That was close. Don't worry my son... I shall hide you from now on.

[Exit stage – Jochebed and baby]

Narrator 2: And so that's what Jochebed did. She hid her **baby** from anyone that would do him harm.

Narrator 1: But, a few months down the line, this was proving to be fairly tricky.

[Enter stage – Jochebed and Miriam]

Jochebed: Oh Miriam! What are we going to do?

Miriam: Well Mum, I was thinking we could go swimming in the **River Nile**, and then we could take a walk past those new five-star pyramids. Apparently they all have a tomb with a view...

Jochebed: No Miriam! I mean... Hold on... Yes! The **River Nile**. Of course. That's where I'll hide my **baby**.

At this point, you could have some people come on with a long sheet of blue material for the river. Or, if you were able to make or buy a backdrop with an image of a river, you could bring this on now to add a bit more to the stage.

Miriam: OK… So does that mean we're going swimming? Should I pack my swimming costume or not?

[Exit stage – Jochebed and Miriam]

Narrator 2: And so, Jochebed made a basket from papyrus and coated it with tar and pitch.

[Enter stage – Jochebed and Miriam. Jochebed places the basket with the baby in the middle of the stage and then exits stage. Miriam crouches at the side of the stage keeping an eye on her brother]

Narrator 1: Then she placed the **baby** in the basket in the **River Nile**, hidden amongst the reeds, out of Pharaoh's soldier's sight.

Narrator 2: Meanwhile, Miriam kept watch to make sure nothing awful happened to her brother.

Narrator 1: But as she sat and watched, a woman approached the **River Nile**.

Miriam: Oh no.

[Enter stage – Princess of Egypt]

Narrator 2: The woman just so happened to be Pharaoh's daughter, the Princess of Egypt!

Miriam: Oh no!

Narrator 1: And the **baby** started crying.

Miriam: Oh no! Please stop crying!

Narrator 2: And the Princess saw the basket.

Miriam: Oh no! Please don't look in the basket!

Narrator 1: And the Princess looked in the basket.

Miriam: Oh no! Please don't hurt him!

Narrator 2: And the Princess who found the crying **baby**… felt sorry for him and she picked him up to comfort him.

Miriam: A-hem! A-he-he-hem! *[Coughing to get the attention of the Princess]*

Princess: Hello, can I help you?

Miriam: Oh, hello. Actually, I was wondering if I could help you! Would you like me to fetch one of the Israelite women who could feed and look after the child for you?

Princess: Yes please. That would be great. Go. Get someone.

[Exit stage – Miriam]

Narrator 1: So, Miriam dashed off home as quick as she could and, dragging her mother by her arm in a hurry, she took her to the Princess, who waited by the **River Nile.**

> It might be a good idea to play the sound of a baby crying in the background at this point in the story.

[Enter stage – Miriam and Jochebed]

Miriam: Mum, look... The princess needs someone to look after this child that she just found.

Jochebed: But that's my...

Miriam: *[Interrupting]* ...Mum! Wink-wink! The princess needs someone – you – to look after the child that she just found. You can look after him in the palace! Away from danger! Yes!?

Jochebed: Oh. I see. Of course. I'm sure I could do that.

[Jochebed takes the baby]

[Exit stage – Princess and Miriam]

Narrator 2: And so, Jochebed took her child to the palace, where she looked after him. The princess raised the **baby** as her own and named him Moses.

Narrator 1: Not only that, but Jochebed got paid!

Jochebed: Really!? Paid!? For looking after my own child! That is brilliant! *[Shouting to Miriam as she exits stage]* Hey, Miriam... Guess what! We can buy a new camel. One that actually has humps!

Narrator 2: The end.

ACT ● DRAMA

MUMMY'S BOY

> **You will need:**
> ◉ A video camera on a tripod
> ◉ A chair
> ◉ A mobile phone

[Enter stage – Ben who begins setting up a video camera on a tripod and positions a chair in front of it]

Ben: *[Muttering to himself]* Set the angle right. Check the viewfinder. All good. Press play and sit down *[presses play and sits down]*. *[To camera]* Hello Mummy, it's your favourite son Ben here. As it's Mother's Day, I thought it would be nice to record you a little video message.

[Enter stage – Jen]

Jen: Hi Ben, what are you up to?

Ben: Argh, Jen. Can't you see I'm recording here?

Jen: Oh, sorry Ben. You carry on, I'll be quiet, I promise.

Ben: Fine, I'll start again. Hello Mummy, it's your favourite son Ben here…

Jen: Seriously? Mummy?

Ben: Shhh! What's wrong with 'Mummy'? She's my Mummy.

Jen: Erm, nothing?

Ben: *[To camera]* Hello Mummy, as it's Mother's Day I thought I'd record you a little video message.

Jen: Ah, that's sweet.

Ben: Shhh!

Jen: Sorry.

Ben: *[To camera]* Mummy, I want to challenge you on all the lies you fed me when I was growing up.

Jen: Ooh, that went downhill fast.

Ben: Number one: you told me that if I sat too close to the TV I would get square eyes. I have since learnt that there is no scientific evidence to substantiate such a claim.

Jen: I'm not sure you're meant to take that literally.

Ben: Number two: you told me carrots make me see in the dark. I have on several occasions attempted to use said vegetable as an affordable alternative to night-vision goggles, with very little success.

Jen: Again, not literal.

Ben: Number three: "Because I said so" is not an acceptable answer. I used it on a test and not only was it wrong but I had to see the teacher.

Jen: That's just stupid!

Ben: Number four: despite eating all my crusts I can assure you that any curl in my hair is purely down to hair product and an excellent hair maintenance routine.

Jen: It's so shiny...

Ben: Number five: I do not...

Jen: *[Interrupting]* Ben, please just stop there a moment. This is your Mum you're...

Ben: *[Interrupting]* You mean 'Mummy'.

Jen: Sorry, this is your 'Mummy' you're talking to. The woman who brought you into this world and sacrificed so much for you. Do you really think you should talk to her like this?

Ben: Yes, I should. She has spun me a web of lies since the day I was born and it has to stop. She must stop the lying!

Jen: Why don't you take a moment to think about those things? Maybe your Mummy didn't want you to damage your eyes so told you to back away from the TV. Maybe carrots and crusts are good for you and she wanted you to be healthy.

Ben: What are you getting at here?

Jen: All I'm saying is, maybe your Mummy cares about you deeply and is just trying to protect you.

Ben: Oh, Jen, you're right. I've been such a fool! My Mummy does just want to protect me. I need to call her right away.

Jen: Ok, good idea.

Ben: *[On the phone]* Mummy, it's your Benjipoos. I just wanted to call and... Yes, Mummy I did promise to call last week but... Well, I've just been busy... Alright, fine I'm sorry... Well, how can I say it like I mean it if I don't really mean it?... Actually, maybe I do want to know what happens when you get to three... No, I'm not giving you lip... No, I don't want to have my mouth washed out with soap, who would want that? Soap is not a food... Well, maybe I don't have anything nice to say...

[Exit stage – Ben]

Jen: I think I'll just borrow this camera. I've got a feeling this video is about to go viral. Ben, wait for me.

[Exit stage – Jen]

ACT ● PUPPETS

GOD CAN'T BE LIKE A MOTHER – HE'S A MAN!

Jack: Hello everyone. So, it turns out that Jill is confused! Which makes a change.

Jill: I am not!

Jack: She is, everyone. Get this, she thinks that God is like... wait for it... a mother!

Jill: Well, He is.

Jack: Don't be ridiculous, Jill. Everyone knows that God is a man.

Jill: If you'll let me explain, Jack.

Jack: I do not want to be involved in your offensive, and quite frankly, heretical, behaviour, thank you very much.

Jill: I just wanted to tell you that...

Jack: Not listening.

Jill: But...

Jack: Not listening, Jill.

Jill: If you let me explain...

Jack: Not listening...

Jill: It all makes sense though if you'll...

Jack: N-O-T lis-ten-ing!

Jill: Then I guess I'll just have to tell everyone what you forgot to do today.

Jack: Oh. Please don't, Jill. It'll make me look really bad. Everyone will think I'm a terrible person.

Jill: Listen to me then.

Jack: Fine. I'm listening.

Jill: So, God is like a mother because...

Jack: This is so ridiculous...

Jill: AHEM!

Jack: Sorry. I'm listening.

Jill: God is like a mother because He has all of the characteristics of a perfect mother.

Jack: Yep. I don't get it.

Jill: Your Mum's pretty nice, Jack. What's good about your Mum?

Jack: Well, she makes me dinner every day. I love dinner. She listens to me when I get home from school, even if I've had a bad day. She gives me a hug sometimes when I'm upset. But she did turn the TV off the other day when I was watching it! And she sent me to my bedroom for getting in trouble at school. She is nice though, most of the time.

Jill: See? Your Mother looks after you. She cares about you. She loves you. I imagine you'd been watching the TV for far too long and she didn't want your eyes to go square. And I imagine she sent you to your room so that hopefully you'll learn to behave in school. It's called discipline, Jack.

Jack: So? What's that got to do with God?

Jill: Well, all of those good things about your Mum – caring and loving and disciplining and wanting the best for you – they are also some of the same good things about God. So, you see, God is like a mother.

Jack: But. No. That's cheating.

Jill: How is that cheating...

Jack: Fine. You're right! Again! At least you didn't tell everyone that thing I forgot to do. Thanks for that.

Jill: What thing? About you not getting your Mum a Mother's Day card?

Jack: Jill! You just told everyone!

Jill: Oops. Sorry. Good job your Mum is forgiving. Come on, let's go. Bye, everyone.

Jack: Bye.

[Exit – Jack and Jill]

JESUS IS ALIVE

4

THEME

The main theme
for this service is **Jesus is alive!**

What an awesome day **Easter Sunday** is.

We have the joy and privilege of celebrating the amazing fact that Jesus did not stay dead, He came back to life and is fully alive now! AND not only that, but He has made it possible for us to live with Him forever too. Wowsers. This is a reason for a celebration.

STORY

The disciples had been
on such an **adventure.**

They had been following Jesus around for years, witnessing amazing things, seeing Him heal, do miracles, be controversial and were challenged in so many ways. Then, just like that He was gone, dead. He was arrested, and killed. They were distraught, they must have been wondering what on earth was going on. How could this amazing man be dead? They were in this state of shock for days and **THEN they are told that He is alive**... Can you imagine what they went through? Wow, what an emotional journey.

IDEAS

The response time in this service
is a **celebration!**

Why not turn this into an extended time and **have a meal together after church** to celebrate that Jesus is alive? You could even have proper party food!

ORDER OF SERVICE

3 MINS **INTRODUCTION / WELCOME**

3 MINS **SING** *Everybody's Welcome*

2 MINS **PRAY** Psalm 9: 1-2 *(The Message)*

4 MINS **SING** *Resurrection Hymn (See, What A Morning)* **MOVE** Flags and ribbons **CREATE** Flower Cross

4 MINS **CREATE** Party hats

8 MINS **ACT** *Jesus appears to the Disciples* **SCRIPT** *see page 69*

3 MINS **TELL 1** Jesus is alive! **SCRIPT** *see page 65*

4 MINS — **SING** *He's My Saviour*

OPTION A

4 MINS

ACT – DRAMA
Unbeatable

SCRIPT *see page 72*

OPTION B

ACT – PUPPETS
Jesus is dead?

SCRIPT *see page 74*

2 MINS — **TELL 2** God's power is stronger than death

SCRIPT *see page 65*

15 MINS — ALL-IN SYNC ALL-IN SYNC ALL-IN SYNC

SING 3-4 songs
about Jesus' resurrection

CREATE
Angels

MOVE
Prepare the party

WRITE
Because Jesus is alive, I can...

DISCUSS
What does it all mean?

THINK
What does it all mean?

3 MINS — **RESPOND** Celebration time!

4 MINS

SING
*Hero Of
The World*

MOVE
Actions

WRITE
What makes
Jesus a hero?

THE FINER DETAIL

SING ▶ MOVE ▶ CREATE

SING

Lead the congregation in *Resurrection Hymn (See What A Morning)******.

MOVE

Create a 'parade' with flags and ribbons and banners. Invite people to wave them or walk around the church triumphantly.

CREATE

Make a cross which is covered in oasis (the green stuff you can stick flowers in). Provide a box full of fresh, colourful flowers and invite those who would like to, to come and stick a flower in the cross to symbolise the new life.

CREATE ⊙ PARTY HATS

The Super-Easy Option Cracker crowns

You need: Cracker party hats (you can buy these in bulk online) – one per person
Pens
Stickers

Invite the congregation to decorate their party hat.

The Easy Option Broadsheet hats

You need: Broadsheet newspapers – one sheet per person
Pens (optional)

▶ Practice how to make a hat from a piece of newspaper – see *www.bigministries.co.uk/theallinthing*.

Lead everyone in creating their hat (and decorating it!).

The Brave Option Create your own crown

You need: Long strips of card – one per person
Scissors
Sticky tape
Stickers / jewels for decoration

Allow time and space for people to design their own crown out of their strip of card.

TELL 1 ● JESUS IS ALIVE

Can you imagine the emotional roller-coaster the disciples were on? They had just had the most incredible three years following Jesus around and seeing amazing things happen. Then He had been arrested, and killed right in front of everyone… They had been mourning His death for three days, and then they were told He was alive again. You wouldn't believe it, would you? But it was so true – **Jesus is alive.** At Easter, we often spend too long focusing on the cross – Good Friday is important, but Sunday is even more important, otherwise there's no point! Jesus is alive, the resurrection changes EVERYTHING!

SING

He's my Saviour*. Find the song at *www.resoundworship.org.*

This is a song that you write with your congregation.

Invite people to shout out (or write down and bring to the front) words to describe Jesus.

Insert the words people use to describe Jesus into the song.

"He is _____, Christ the Lord."

TELL 2 ● GOD IS MORE POWERFUL THAN DEATH

Death is unbeatable – and yet God is so powerful He has made it beatable. He has not just beaten it, but He has made it possible for us to beat it too.

The resurrection shows us, not only that God is amazingly powerful, but it shows us the start of everything getting fixed. One day there will be no more death, no more pain, no more sadness… the resurrection is the sign of this future hope.

Jesus is alive!

ALL-IN SYNC ALL-IN SYNC ALL-IN SYNC

SING

Sing a few songs about **Jesus being alive!**

Come People Of The Risen King
Keith Getty, Kristyn Getty,
Stuart Townend

For This Purpose
Graham Kendrick

He Has Risen Noel Richards

Led Like A Lamb Graham Kendrick

Thine Be The Glory Edmond Budry,
Richard Hoyle, Georg Friedrich Handel

Glorious Day (Living He Loved Me)
Michael Bleecker, John Wilbur Chapman,
Mark Hall

Mighty To Save (Everyone Needs Compassion) Ben Fielding, Reuben Morgan

Happy Day Tim Hughes

Copyright details for these songs can be found on page 108.

CREATE • Angels

Depending on your resources and abilities (!), there are a couple of options.

The Paper Plate Option

You will need:

- Paper plates
- Marker pens
- Glitter
- A stapler
- Sticky-tak

Draw the outline of an angel (see below) on the eating side of your plate.

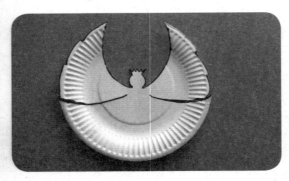

Turn the plate over and decorate.

Bring the bottom half pieces together and staple together. Add a blob of sticky-tak to the front of your angel to enable it to stand up.

During the activity, or when the activity is finished, talk about:

How do you think the women felt when an angel was at the tomb and not Jesus?

Do you think angels are scary?

The Sock Puppet Option

You need:

- White socks
- Glittery pipe cleaners
- Googly eyes OR white / black circle stickers
- Paper for wings
- Glitter
- Scissors
- Sticky tape

Cut out a wing shape from paper, and decorate with glitter on both sides.

Make a halo with the glittery pipe cleaner by making a circle on the end of a stick. Then fold the circle down so it is at ninety degrees to the stick.

Put the sock onto your hand and push the toe part into the middle of your hand to make the mouth (add a tongue if you want!)

Using glue, attach the wings to the sock at the back of your hand. Attach the halo to a similar area, allowing it to stick up above your hand (gaffer tape may be effective at attaching).

More decorating can be done with glitter / stickers and permanent markers!

THE FINER DETAIL   **JESUS IS ALIVE**

MOVE • Prepare the party!

You will need:

- Balloons
- String
- Streamers
- Party poppers
- *optional* Party bags and small items to go in them.
- *optional* Cakes or sweets!

The move zone are going to be preparing for the response time – we are going to celebrate **Jesus is alive** with a mini party.

Blow up the balloons. Have some loose for 'playing with' and some on string, hung around the church.

Decorate the church with the streamers, and spread the party poppers around so people can use them later.

If you are going to make party bags, then these will need assembling also, and cakes put out on plates.

As the preparation goes on, talk about:

What does it mean to us that Jesus is alive?

What difference does it actually make?

WRITE

Make sure you have some nice writing paper, nice pens and Bibles available.

"Because Jesus is alive, I can…"

Write a poem with this as your starter line.

DISCUSS

Someone leading the discussion is ideal.

Use the worksheet on page 76 as your discussion starter. Print out copies for people.

Other questions:

What does it mean to us that Jesus is alive?

What difference does it actually make?

THINK

Make available: Bibles, cushions, ear defenders, paper, pens and even mp3 players with headphones.

Use the worksheet on page 76 as the basis for **THINK**. Print out copies for people.

Other questions:

What does it mean to us that Jesus is alive?

What difference does it actually make?

RESPOND

We are going to celebrate as **Resurrection People!**

Put some party music on and release the balloons to play with, eat cake if you're providing it and invite people to wear their party hats and have some fun celebrating the fact that **Jesus is alive!! WOO HOO!**

SING ▶ MOVE ▶ WRITE

SING

Hero of the World* – this song is on *The All-In Thing Songs* CD.

MOVE

▶ Actions – see *www.bigministries.co.uk/theallinthing*.

WRITE

Invite people to write down some truths about Jesus – what makes Him a hero? Why is that different from a superhero?

PRAY

It's not on the order of service, but do close the service with prayer!

ACT ● STORY

JESUS APPEARS TO HIS DISCIPLES ● LUKE 24

Characters:

- Narrator 1
- Narrator 2
- Jesus
- Woman 1
- Woman 2
- Disciple 1
- Disciple 2

Teach the audience these **trigger words** *before reading the story:*

Jesus is alive	*Cheer!*
Hands	*Hold your hands out and shout,* **"hands!"**
Feet	*Point at your feet and shout,* **"feet!"**
Angels	*An angelic* **"laaaa"** *(some harmonies would be good).*

Narrator 1: Jesus was dead. His body had been wrapped in linen and laid in a tomb and a huge stone had been rolled across the entrance.

[Enter stage – Women 1 and 2]

Narrator 2: It was now the first day of the week and some women, who had known Jesus, went to the tomb. But, on arriving, they saw that the stone had been rolled away from the entrance.

Women 1 and 2: Look! The stone's been rolled away from the entrance!

Narrator 1: And when they entered the tomb, they found that Jesus' body had gone.

Women 1 and 2: Jesus' body has gone!

Narrator 2: Suddenly, two **angels**, shining as bright as lightning, appeared before the women, who lay in fear with their faces to the ground.

> The angels that appear could be shown as two bright lights shining from stage. Perhaps two bright lights shining behind a backdrop of white material.

Narrator 1: The angels told them that Jesus had risen from the dead, just as He said He would, and then, the **angels** left...

Woman 1: Jesus is alive!

Woman 2: Come on, let's go and tell the disciples...

Narrator 2: And so, off the women went to tell the disciples about all they had heard and seen. But the disciples did not believe them.

[Exit stage – Women 1 and 2]

[Enter stage – Disciples 1 and 2, shortly followed by Jesus. March on the spot, facing the audience. Disciples 1 and 2 either side of Jesus]

Narrator 1: Not long after the angels had appeared, two of the disciples were walking along a road, just outside the City of Jerusalem. Jesus started walking with them, but they were kept from recognising Him.

Narrator 2: It was only later that evening, when Jesus broke bread and gave thanks before eating a meal, that the two disciples recognised that it was Jesus who had been with them all day...

Disciple 1: It's you!

Disciple 2: Jesus is...

Disciple 1: Jesus is...

Disciples 1 and 2: Jesus is alive!

[Exit stage – Jesus]

Narrator 1: But Jesus disappeared from their sight. The disciples then ran off to tell the others.

Disciple 2: Come on! let's go back to Jerusalem and tell the others that **Jesus is alive!**

Narrator 2: The two disciples travelled back along the seven mile long road, back to Jerusalem. They arrived at a house where all of the disciples were together discussing the whereabouts of Jesus' body and whether or not **angels** had appeared to the women.

> If you have a clear, hidden and accessible behind stage area, when the disciples run back to Jerusalem, they could run across the stage several times, coming on from the same side each time until arriving at the disciples' house.

[Enter stage – other disciples]

Disciple 1: *[Talking to all of the disciples]* You chaps will never guess what...

[All in one breath, both very excitedly talking at the same time and both finishing on the word 'Jesus' at the same time]

Disciple 1: We were walking along the road and then this guy turned up and walked with us, but we didn't know it was Jesus, and we talked about amazing things and then we stopped for some food and then He broke bread and then we realised it was Jesus...

Disciple 2: It was crazy! We just saw Jesus, He's not dead anymore. I was all like, no way, it's Jesus, and then I was all like, weird, why didn't I know it was Jesus before, but He broke some bread and then He was gone, just after we realised it was in fact, Jesus...

Disciples 3: Wait. What are you talking about!?

Disciples 1 and 2: Jesus is alive!

[Enter stage – Jesus (appearing in the middle of all of the disciples)]

Narrator 1: And as the disciples continued to discuss this, Jesus appeared right in the middle of them! The disciples trembled with fear thinking they were seeing a ghost.

Disciples: ARRRRGH! A GHOST!

Jesus: Peace be with you. Why are you frightened? Look at the nail marks that remain in my **hands** and my **feet**. It's me – Jesus. Touch me and see for yourself that I'm real.

Narrator 2: The disciples were near enough speechless. They looked at Jesus' **hands** and they looked at Jesus' **feet.**

Jesus and the disciples could join in with the "hands" and "feet" trigger words from stage in order to give a bit more 'oomph'.

Narrator 1: They saw the nail marks in His **hands** and in His **feet** and they saw and felt that He was real. They were definitely not imagining Him. He was standing right in front of them, in the flesh; **Jesus was alive!**

Disciples: It's really you!

Narrator 2: Jesus then spoke to them all saying...

Jesus: I am going to send you what my Father has promised, but wait here in the city until you have received the Holy Spirit.

Narrator 1: So the disciples remained in Jerusalem and they waited just as Jesus had told them to. They were all filled with joy at realising that **Jesus is alive!**

UNBEATABLE

> **You will need:**
> ◉ A 'Ben Wins' card

[Ben enters looking for Jen]

Ben: Jen! Jen! JEEEEEEEEEEEEEEEEEEEN! Jen, Jen, Jen! Jen, Jen, Jen! *[Jen enters and watches Ben as he continues calling for her]* Jen, Jen, Jen, Jen, Jen, Jen, Jen, Jen, Jen, Jen, Jen, Jen, JEEEEEEEEEEEEEEEEEEEN!

Jen: Yes?

Ben: Oh, there you are, Jen.

Jen: Yes, here I am. What can I do for you?

Ben: I need you to play. Right now.

Jen: Play what?

Ben: Beatable Unbeatable.

Jen: What?

Ben: Beatable Unbeatable. It's the most amazing game – I've just invented it – and it is your duty and your privilege to now play the game with me.

Jen: And it's called… Beatable…

Ben: Unbeatable. Beatable Unbeatable. You give me a list of different things and I tell you whether they are beatable or unbeatable.

Jen: Ok, sounds simple enough. An egg.

Ben: Beata… Hey, take it seriously!

Jen: Sorry. Couldn't resist. Erm, a tank.

Ben: Beatable.

Jen: A rhinoceros.

Ben: Beatable.

Jen: Tyrannosaurus Rex.

Ben: Beatable.

Jen: My Dad.

Ben: Beatable.

Jen: Your Dad.

Ben: Unbeatable.

Jen: How come your Dad is unbeatable and my...

Ben: *[Interrupting]* Unbeatable.

Jen: I'm pretty sure on sports day my Dad beat...

Ben: *[Interrupting]* Unbeatable.

Jen: Fine. Blue whale.

Ben: Beatable.

Jen: Steel.

Ben: Beatable.

Jen: Spiderman.

Ben: Beatable.

Jen: Giant octopus.

Ben: Beatable.

Jen: Manchester United.

Ben: Beatable.

Jen: Concrete.

Ben: Beatable.

Jen: Unicorns.

Ben: Unbeatable.

Jen: The sun.

Ben: Beatable.

Jen: Ooh, I've got a good one. Death!

Ben: Unbeatable. Wait no, beatable. I mean unbeatable... or is it beatable? Ooooh, I don't know.

Jen: Does that mean I win?

Ben: No, because I play my 'Ben Wins' card. *[Ben pulls out a card and holds it up]*

Jen: You can't do that.

Ben: I can. It's my game, my rules.

Jen: That's just stupid. The 'Ben Wins' card is...

Ben: *[Interrupting]* Unbeatable. I win, oh yeah. It doesn't matter anyway. I have a new game now. It's called Blendable Unblendable. You give me a list of things and I tell you whether they'd be good in a smoothie.

Jen: Ben, that's not a good game. I'm going to go home now.

[Exit Jen followed by Ben]

Ben: You don't know until you've tried it. Come on. Giant octopus. Blendable unblendable? Unicorns. Blendable unblendable? I was gonna win anyway...

ACT ⬤ PUPPETS

JESUS IS DEAD?

[Jill on stage. Enter – Jack, wailing pathetically]

Jill: Woah there Jack, what's wrong?

[Jack ignores Jill and continues wailing]

Jill: Jack? *[Jill tries to get Jack's attention]*

Jack: *[Wailing]* He's dead!

Jill: Who's dead?

Jack: Jesus. Weren't you listening? Jesus is dead!

Jill: Oh yeah. I guess that is kinda sad.

Jack: Kinda sad? Kinda sad? It's the worst thing to happen since last Thursday.

[Pause]

Jill: I know you want me to ask you what happened last Thursday…

Jack: Well, what happened was…

Jill: *[Interrupting]* … But I'm not going to.

Jack: *[Speaking quickly so Jill can't stop him]* … Someone stole my sandwich from my lunchbox at school. It was Marmite and jam. My absolute favouritest sandwich in the whole world of all time ever.

Jill: I'm going to go out on a limb here, Jack, and suggest that this news, Jesus being dead, is even worse than that.

Jack: Maybe you're right, Jill. And you know what makes it even worse?

Jill: What's that, Jack?

Jack: The fact that it happened on Good Friday. How ironic is that?

Jill: Uh, Jack…

Jack: Of all the days for Jesus to die on.

Jill: Jack.

Jack: I mean, any other day would have been better.

Jill: *[Raising her voice a little]* Jack. It's called Good Friday because it's the day Jesus died.

[Pause]

Jack: What? That doesn't make any sense at all Jill. Why would they call it Good Friday?

Jill: Yeah, now that you come to mention it, that does seem a little odd.

Jack: It should be called Bad Friday. Or Horrendous Friday. Or Miserable Friday. Or Just-Simply-Awful Friday.

Jill: Or, [pause for effect] Egregious Friday.

Jack: Yeah.

Jill: That means really, really, really bad.

Jack: Yeah. I knew that. [Making it clear he did not]

Jill: Even I, with my massive brain, don't know why anyone would call such a terrible day Good Friday. Shall we ask Alex?

Jack: OK! Let's call him.

[Perhaps get the audience to help summon Alex. Too cheesy?]

[Alex enters]

Alex: Hi guys. How are you?

Jack: We're really, really confused.

Jill: I'm only slightly confused.

Jack: Why is the day that Jesus died called Good Friday? And not Egre... Egre... mous...

Jill: Egregious Friday.

Jack: It's just the worst day I can think of.

Alex: That is a very good question. Well the name Good Friday actually comes from God Friday. It's got sort of changed over the years.

Jack: God Friday?

Alex: And although it seems very sad, it's totally not the end of the story.

Jill: Why? What happens next?

Alex: Well you have to think forward to Sunday.

Jack: What happens on Sunday?

Alex: Sunday is Easter Day. And that's the day we remember that Jesus came back from the dead!

Jill and Jack together: Back from the dead?

Jill: Things are certainly starting to look up a bit.

Jack: So Jesus didn't stay dead?

Alex: No. God raised Him from the dead.

Jill: Wow. God is so powerful even death can't stop Him.

Alex: Pretty impressive, eh?

Jack: I'm certainly feeling much more cheerful now. In fact I think I want to... celebrate. [Singing] Celebrate good times, come on!

Jill: Thanks Alex, for helping Jack to understand. He was really confused in his tiny pea sized brain.

Jack: I'm going to celebrate more by eating the Marmite and jam sandwich I found at the bottom of my bag this morning.

[Jack exits singing Celebrate. Jill and Alex follow]

JESUS DIED AND CAME BACK TO LIFE. HOW DOES THAT SAVE ME?

If Jesus has beaten death, then why do we still die?

BIG STORY

Jesus was born, He lived on earth as a boy. He grew up to be a man and never did anything wrong, He always treated people well.

BUT He was arrested and killed... Three days later **Jesus was alive again!** WOAH!

Matthew, Mark, Luke & John.

What do you think the **women's faces** looked like when they found Jesus' tomb was **empty?**

DRAW THEM HERE!

Who's your favourite superhero?

Who's your **hero?**

What's the difference between a **SUPERHERO** and a **HERO?**

CHECK IT OUT...

Draw yourself as a mini **SUPERHERO!**

DICTIONARY CORNER

SUPERHERO A kind, but made-up character with special super-powers. They hide their identity (usually with some sort of super-cool outfit).

HERO Someone **real** who is admired because of the things they do (and their love and bravery). No outfit required!

BONUS BIG QUESTION:

Jesus was God on Earth... So did God die?

What does it mean?

RIGHTEOUSNESS

CHECK IT OUT

ROMANS 6:4

What do you think of this verse?

P.S. It's OK to say we don't really know, but just believe it does!

CHALLENGE!

How many words can you get from these letters?

DEATH AND RESURRECTION

tree

sure

In the Bible – Romans 6:23 – it tells us that the price of sin to us all is death... ☹

So, when Jesus died (after no sin in His life), it was like He took all the sin and mess from the whole world with Him – so He paid the price for everyone.

Jesus coming back to life and beating death (woohoo!) was the start of God's super-fix-it plan for the world. (It was as if Jesus left all the mess behind in the grave when He came back to life.)

IT'S A HOLY MYSTERY

To be honest, it is a complete mystery how this actually works, and people with mega brains have been trying to explain it for hundreds of years (and not really succeeding!). All we know is that somehow what Jesus did gives us the opportunity to live with God (just like we were meant to), and also to do that forever!

Jesus died and came back to life, how does that save me?

SO...

PRAY!

Thank Jesus for what He did to save the world (and you!)

AMEN!

There is no greater hero... Jesus, the Hero of the World! ♪

ALL -IN

THE HOLY SPIRIT'S POWER

5

THEME

The main theme today is **the Holy Spirit's power.**

The Holy Spirit is not something that is often talked about when we are **All-In** together. It's excitingly risky because we don't know what God will do. The Holy Spirit is unpredictable, and really exciting!

Let's pray that during this service people will have a real experience of the Holy Spirit, in a way that makes sense to them.

STORY

The story of **Pentecost** is quite a dramatic one, and hopefully the script within this book will help you to convey the frustration of the waiting disciples and **the excitement as the Holy Spirit arrives** and gives them power, which is so much more than they could ever imagine.

Jesus had told the disciples that they needed to wait for Him to send them His Spirit, which they did, and He fulfilled His promise to them. I think sometimes we are not patient enough, we want instant results and want God's power NOW so we can go and change the world. God will send us His power, but it might not be when we think and it might not be in the way that we expect. THAT is what's so exciting!

IDEAS

Why not use this **All-In service** as a way to kick-start a series across the whole church looking at the **Holy Spirit?**

When you're not All-In together, you can study who He is and what He does.

ORDER OF SERVICE

3 MINS · **INTRODUCTION / WELCOME**

3 MINS · **SING** *Everybody's Welcome*

2 MINS · **PRAY** Psalm 32: 11 *(The Message)*

4 MINS · **SING** *Come You Thankful People* · **MOVE** Signs

3 MINS · **CREATE** Fan

8 MINS · **ACT** *Pentecost* · **SCRIPT** *see page 85*

3 MINS · **TELL 1** Great power, great responsibility · **SCRIPT** *see page 80*

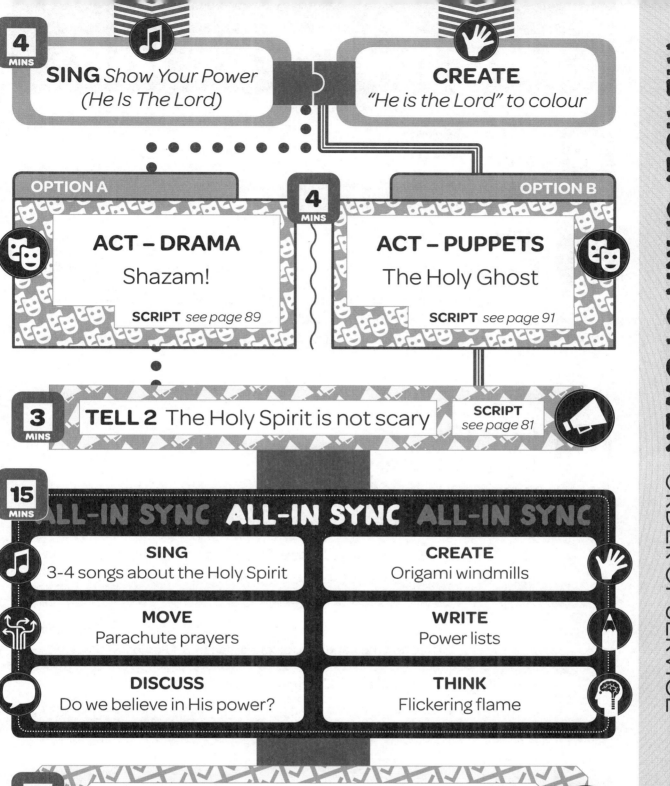

4 MINS

SING *Show Your Power (He Is The Lord)*

CREATE *"He is the Lord" to colour*

OPTION A

ACT – DRAMA

Shazam!

SCRIPT *see page 89*

4 MINS

OPTION B

ACT – PUPPETS

The Holy Ghost

SCRIPT *see page 91*

3 MINS

TELL 2 The Holy Spirit is not scary

SCRIPT *see page 81*

15 MINS

ALL-IN SYNC ALL-IN SYNC ALL-IN SYNC

SING
3-4 songs about the Holy Spirit

CREATE
Origami windmills

MOVE
Parachute prayers

WRITE
Power lists

DISCUSS
Do we believe in His power?

THINK
Flickering flame

3 MINS

RESPOND What are we going to do with the Holy Spirit's power? Adapt your fan

4 MINS

SING
I Believe

MOVE
Actions

CREATE
Make your mark

THE FINER DETAIL

SING ▶ MOVE

SING

Lead the congregation in *Come You Thankful People**.
Find the song at *www.resoundworship.org*.

MOVE

▶ Sign language on the chorus – see *www.bigministries.co.uk/theallinthing*

This song is so easy to pick up for people, even for non-readers in the congregation, as the line "To praise the one true God" repeats many times. You could even lead this song as a leader/ response song, so only invite the congregation to sing that repeated line.

CREATE ◉ FAN

The Super-Easy Option Fan

You need: A4 paper – one piece per person

Fold the piece of paper as a simple concertina to create a fan.

The Slightly-More-Complicated Option Fan of flames

You need: A4 paper – one piece per person
Red, orange and yellow pens

Invite people to draw flames on their piece of paper on both sides. Then fold the paper into a concertina fan of flames!

The Mega-Complicated Option Origami fan

(Only try this if you're sure you can explain it AND your congregation will manage – you don't want to immediately alienate everyone because they feel like they can't do it!)

You need: Squares of paper – one per person

▶ You will need to practice making this fan!
See *www.bigministries.co.uk/theallinthing* for help.

TELL 1 ◉ GREAT POWER, GREAT RESPONSIBILITY

Show a clip from *Spider-Man*, starring Tobey Maguire. It is where Uncle Ben tells Peter that "with great power comes great responsibility" (search for this on Youtube!).

It's so exciting. The power that was at work in the story we just saw – the Holy Spirit – is still the same today, and is available for all of us. We can have this great power working in us. We just have to ask God.

We then, though, have a great responsibility to follow what He wants us to do, and to do God's work.

It's more than just asking for the Holy Spirit and having a nice warm fuzzy feeling. If we ask for the Holy Spirit, He could ask us to go anywhere or do anything... and it might not be so warm and fuzzy! But at least the Holy Spirit goes with us!

Teach the congregation the phrase with accompanying signs – see *www.bigministries.co.uk/theallinthing*.

With great power comes great responsibility.

SING  CREATE

SING

Lead the congregation in singing *Show Your Power (He is the Lord)* *****.

CREATE

On a large roll of paper write HE IS THE LORD in large letters. Invite those who want to, to come and colour these in during this song. You could then stick this up on a wall somewhere.

TELL 2 ● THE HOLY SPIRIT IS NOT SCARY

Powerful things can quite often be a bit scary. Unknown things can often be a bit scary. The Holy Spirit is very unknown and also very powerful. This could mean that He is scary. But let me assure you, He is not.

The Holy Spirit, as well as being powerful, is described as a comforter, a dove, a teacher, as the oil of anointing, as a gift and as a shepherd.

God gives us His Holy Spirit to be with us and to guide us.

Recap: with **great power** comes **great responsibility.**

 Learn: The Holy Spirit is not scary!
(For signs, see *www.bigministries.co.uk/theallinthing*)

SING

Sing a few songs about The Holy Spirit's Power.

He Is The Lord (Show Your Power)
Kevin Prosch

Spirit Break Out Ben Bryant, Myles
Dhillon, Luke Hellebronth, Tim Hughes

Open The Eyes Of My Heart
Paul Baloche

Consuming Fire Tim Hughes

Strength Will Rise (Everlasting God)
Brenton Brown, Ken Riley

Holy Spirit We Welcome You
Chris Bowater

Spirit Of The Living God Fall Afresh
Daniel Iverson

Copyright details for these songs can be found on page 108.

CREATE • Origami Windmills

You will need:

- ◉ Squares of card
- ◉ Strong straws / sticks / pipe cleaners for the stems
- ◉ Glue
- ◉ Split Pins
- ◉ Stickers / tissue paper / decorations

▶ For the template to make a windmill with your square of paper, see *www.bigministries.co.uk/theallinthing.*

Decorate your square. Attach it with a split pin to your 'stem'.

To talk about during the activity:

Why do you think the Holy Spirit is compared to the wind?

MOVE • Parachute Prayers

You will need:

- ◉ A parachute
- ◉ Possibly a separate room so as to not be too much of a distraction

Invite the people in this zone to split into two groups.

Group 1 are to lie on the floor on their backs with their eyes closed.

Group 2 are to stand around the parachute and hold it over those lying down.

Group 2 should wave the parachute over the others whilst praying for the Holy Spirit to come and do whatever He wants to do.

Allow this to take a good amount of time. Then swap over groups.

Get feedback as to what God has been doing.

THE FINER DETAIL **THE HOLY SPIRIT'S POWER**

WRITE

Make sure you have some nice writing paper, nice pens and Bibles available.

Option 1

Write some lists of power. Constructive Power and Destructive Power. Think about the sort of power that the Holy Spirit has – where does it fit?

Option 2

Create a collection of words (that looks like a crossword – so they all join up) describing God's power.

DISCUSS

Someone leading the discussion is ideal.

Why do we not always expect the miraculous?

Do we not believe the Holy Spirit is powerful enough?

Have you ever witnessed or experienced the sort of power we heard about in the story?

THINK

Make available: Bibles, cushions, ear defenders, paper, pens and even mp3 players with headphones.

Either set up actual candles for people to watch, or a screen with a visual of candles or flames flickering.

Watch the flames. Think about the Holy Spirit.
Who is He? What does He do?
Why do we compare Him to flames of fire?

RESPOND

There's a few options here depending on where you think your congregation are at.

Option 1 Invite the Holy Spirit to come

Ask everyone to sit (provide the fidget toys for those who need them to be able to sit), close their eyes, perhaps hold their hands out and wait.

Simply pray for God to send His Holy Spirit.

See what happens!

Option 2 WRITE

Invite people to write or draw their own prayers (on their fan) asking God to send them His Spirit.

Option 3 MOVE

Invite people to write or draw a prayer for the Holy Spirit to come like a rushing wind on their fan. Then lead people in turning their fan into an aeroplane. Then all throw the planes to symbolise God's Spirit moving amongst us.

SING ▶ MOVE ▶ CREATE

SING

*I Believe** – this song is on *The All-In Thing Songs* CD.

MOVE

▶ Actions – see *www.bigministries.co.uk/theallinthing.*

CREATE

Have a large WE BELIEVE on paper. Provide ink pads (and wet wipes) for people to add their fingerprint onto the board. Invite people to do the fingerprint if they believe in the power of the Holy Sprit and are happy to let His power work in them.

PRAY

It's not on the order of service, but do close the service with prayer!

ACT ● STORY
PENTECOST ● ACTS 2

Characters:
- Narrator 1
- Narrator 2
- Peter
- John
- Father Christmas
- Pizza Delivery Person

You will need:
- A fairly powerful fan
- Confetti
- Paper streamers

To visually create the sense of the Holy Spirit filling the room, attempt this:

Attach streamers to the fan. Place the fan on the floor in the centre/back of the stage pointing up at a ninety-degree angle. Place the confetti in the path of where the air from the fan will blow. Place a board in front of the fan when you first turn the fan on to allow the fan to run at full power before blowing the confetti. Remove the board and watch the confetti blow all around the place. We recommend trialling this beforehand in order to get it right.

Teach the audience these **trigger words** *before reading the story:*

Wait / waiting / waited	*Say* **"why are we waiting?"**
Pray / prayed	*Say* **"amen!"**

[Enter stage – Peter and John]

Peter: John! It's been days now. Literally, days!

John: Peter, I know it's been days. But, He said to **wait**.

Narrator 1: For a few days now, Peter and John and the rest of the disciples had been **waiting**.

John and Peter: We know!

Narrator 2: But who said to **wait**, and for what, and why and when and where and... well?

John: It was Jesus.

Peter: Jesus said to **wait**.

John: Just before He went up into the sky.

Peter: Wait. We need to **wait**!

> If you wanted to, you could place a huge clock face on the stage that John and Peter could stare at as they wait.

John: We need to **wait** for something... for someone... That He's going to send us.

Narrator 1: And so that is what they did. Just as Jesus had said.

Peter: John...

John: Yes, Peter?...

Peter: Is it time yet?

John: How should I know?

Peter: Let's play Scrabble... I'm so bored! Or Twister... I can definitely beat you at Twister. I'm so limber.

[Peter contorts himself into a Twister-like position]

John: Oh yeah? You think you can beat me, "John, the king of contortion"? I'll beat you, hands down, no competition.

[John now begins twisting into strange positions as they both compete with each other]

Peter: You look ridiculous.

Narrator 2: Peter and John did NOT play games while they **waited**.

[Peter and John stand up and look embarrassed. They compose themselves and sit down behaving themselves]

Narrator 1: They **prayed**.

Peter: I told you we should be **praying**.

John: No you didn't.

Peter: Did too!

Narrator 1: Nor did they argue!... As I said, they **prayed**, as they **waited** for that which Jesus had promised them.

[Heads down in their hands, praying]

Peter: John... *[Glancing up while still in a 'prayer position']*

John: Yes, Peter?

Peter: What do you think Jesus has us holding on for?

John: I'm not sure, but I'm certain that it's going to be really good.

Peter: John...

John: Yes, Peter?...

Peter: I think it could be Father Christmas...

[Enter stage – Father Christmas]

Father Christmas: Ho Ho Ho!

> You could play a Christmas pop song here, just as Father Christmas walks in.

Narrator 2: It was NOT Father Christmas!

Father Christmas: Ho Ho… No…

[Exit stage – Father Christmas]

Peter: John…

John: Yes, Peter?…

Peter: Do you think it could be a pizza?… I love pizza.

[Enter stage – Pizza Delivery Person]

Pizza delivery Person: Pizza for Peter!

[Exit stage – Pizza delivery Person]

Narrator 1: It was NOT a pizza.

Peter: John…

John: What!? What is it, Peter? What do you want to say? Do I think it's a birthday gift for you? A tree for your garden? A camel, a donkey, a horse? No! No, I do not think it is any of those things!

Peter: [sulking] … I don't need a donkey anyway. Got loads.

> After John's mini rant, a person could walk onto stage with a small tree and a person dressed as a donkey and a camel and a horse… And then freeze and walk off as John glares at them.

Narrator 2: And so they **waited**… And **waited**… And **prayed**… And **waited**… And **prayed** some more… Until…

[Peter and John stand up quickly with a gasp of excitement]

Narrator 1: Not yet.

[Peter and John sit down again]

Narrator 2: Until…

[Peter and John stand up quickly with a gasp of excitement]

Narrator 1: Not yet…

[Peter and John sit down again]

Narrator 2: Until…

[Peter and John stand up quickly with a gasp of excitement]

Narrator 1: It happened! A sound from heaven, like that of a strong and violent wind, filled the house that the disciples were in!

[Turn fan on which blows the confetti everywhere. Attach streamers to the fan for added effect]

> Here, you could play a sound effect of a strong and violent wind to go along with the fan and confetti.

Narrator 2: And then… all of the disciples saw what appeared to be tongues of fire resting on each others heads. Not only that, but they could all speak in different languages…

Peter: Bonjour!

John: Auf Wiedersehen!

Narrator 1: As word spread around the towns and cities of what was going on, people came from all around. The people from the surrounding villages were amazed to hear the disciples speaking their language.

Narrator 2: With thousands of people now gathered, Peter stood in front of them and told them all about the incredible story of Jesus.

Peter: John...

John: Yes, Peter...

Peter: Then what happened?

John: Well, Peter, three thousand people joined the church that day...

Peter: Wow, really?

John: Yes. You were there.

Peter: Oh yeah... John...

John: Yes, Peter? What is it now?

Peter: We'd better go, church starts in ten minutes.

John: You're right! GO!

[Exit stage – Peter and John]

Narrator 1: The end.

ACT ◉ DRAMA

SHAZAM!

You will need:

◉ A 'superhero' mask, which Ben wears throughout.

[Ben is on stage concentrating with his eyes closed and holding two fingers to his temple]

[Enter stage – Jen]

Jen: Hi, everyone. Has anyone seen Ben this morning? Oh, never mind, here he is.

[Jen, confused by his posture, stares at Ben for a while, whilst waving her hand in front of his face]

Jen: Erm... Ben? Ben. BEN!

Ben: Shh! It is of cosmic importance that I concentrate.

Jen: Yes, of course but what on earth are you up to this time?

Ben: *[Opening his eyes]* Urgh. If you must know, I am training my super-powers so I can change the world!

Jen: Really? Because it kind of looks like you're trying not to wet yourself.

Ben: Ha ha. Very funny, Jen! You can laugh all you want but I have super powers and I am going to change the world.

Jen: Ben, you are certainly different from the rest of us but I'm pretty sure you don't have super-powers.

Ben: Well, that's where you are wrong because I do have super-powers.

Jen: If that's true, what super-powers do you have?

Ben: I can use my mind to do things.

Jen: *[Pause]* Oh, OK. I feel like I should make a joke about that, but I also think you've made it just too easy... So I won't. What kind of things can you do with your mind?

Ben: Well, OK, for one I can control wild animals. For example, as we speak, I am protecting everyone here from stampeding elephants using only the power of my mind.

Jen: Ben, there are hardly any elephants in the country, let alone stampeding through *[insert town / city name]*.

Ben: I know, right? Pretty powerful stuff, huh? Shazam!

Jen: Oh brother. So, is that the full extent of your super-powers?

Ben: Oh no, Jen. There's more than that. I can melt ice using the power of my mind.

Jen: Really?

Ben: If I focus really hard, yes... but it can take a while and it works better in the summer.

Jen: Oh come on, Ben, you can't seriously believe...

Ben: *[Interrupting]* Oh, also, I can read my own mind.

Jen: That's not really that impressive.

Ben: OK, how about this... I have the power to read your mind.

Jen: That would be more impressive.

Ben: Think of a vegetable that rhymes with parrot.

[Ben closes eyes and holds two fingers to his temple]

Ben: Carrot, right? Shazam!

Jen: That's just ridiculous. Ben, I really don't believe your super-powers are real.

Ben: *[Closing eyes and holding two fingers to temple again]* I am sensing disbelief. Am I right?

Jen: Yes, Ben.

Ben: Shazam!

Jen: No, Ben. No Shazam. I literally just told you out loud that I didn't believe you had super-powers.

Ben: Did you, Jen?

Jen: Yes.

Ben: But did you really, Jen?

Jen: Yes. Really.

Ben: Oh. So, I don't have super-powers?

Jen: No, Ben. You don't.

Ben: Well, that's sad. I really wanted to have super-powers because I wanted to change the world and now I can't because I don't have super-powers anymore.

Jen: Anymore? Erm... never mind. Ben, I'm not sure you actually need super-powers to change the world.

Ben: Really?

Jen: Really. I think you already have all the power you need to make a difference in this world. You can use every ability you have to change the world.

Ben: Yay! Can I still wear a costume?

Jen: Not if you want people to take you seriously.

Ben: Shazam! A costume it is!

[Exit Jen and Ben still talking]

Ben: Jen, do you think I could borrow a pair of your tights?

Jen: I don't think so.

Ben: Do you think I could borrow a pair of your mum's tights instead then? Or maybe your Grannie's?

Jen: I really don't think so, and maybe we should have this conversation when we're not at church. Or maybe never. That'd be good as well.

ACT ⦿ PUPPETS

THE HOLY GHOST

[Jill is offstage, dressed up as a ghost using a sheet. Enter – Jack in a panic]

Jack: Ahhhhhhh... HELP ME!

Jill: *[In a ghostly voice]* Oooooooooh. I'm the Holy Spirit... Ooooooh.

Jack: Alex, Alex, help!

[Enter stage – Alex]

Alex: What's happening?

Jill: *[In a ghostly voice]* Thou shalt give me sweets.

Jack: But I haven't got any sweets.

[Enter – Jill]

Alex: Jill, What are you doing?

Jill: I'm not Jill, I'm the ooooooh Holy Spirit... Sweets... Sweets.

Jack: *[Still scared]* You can have my coat, but I've not got any sweeties.

Alex: No, Jack... it's just Jill messing around.

Jill: Nooooo, it's not Jill, it's *[Alex pulls off the sheet]* me, the Ho ... Jill, it is me.

Jack: Oh, Jill, it's you.

Jill: Yeah, I thought that would work to get sweets. It didn't.

Alex: Jill, Why would you dress up as a ghost pretending to be the Holy Spirit?

Jack: Yeah, Jill.

Jill: I kind of thought that it was worth a shot – the Holy Spirit is scary, so I could pretend to be a scary ghost and get stuff!

Alex: The Holy Spirit isn't scary, Jill.

Jill: Oh?

Alex: Sometimes He does things that are a bit unusual, but there's nothing to be scared of. He helps us in our lives – gives us God's power.

Jack: That's not scary.

Alex: I know. He also speaks to us – We just have to make sure we're listening – There's loads of stories in the Bible where the Spirit spoke to people and then did some amazing things when they did what He said!

Jack: How are we supposed to listen for Him speaking?

Jill: You could start by no more talking, Jack.

Jack: Hey!

Alex: You could try sitting quietly and ask Him to speak to you, then wait for a bit. Sometimes it might help to have a Bible with you, or some paper and pens.

Jill: That doesn't sound too hard.

Alex: No.

Jack: Let's give it a go. Jill, let's go sit and be quiet.

Jill: Sounds good to me.

[Exit – all]

Jill: *[Offstage]* Ooh. This is a comfy chair.

Jack: *[As if through non-moving lips]* Jill, go and make Jack some jam sandwiches... this is the Holy Spirit speaking.

Jill: Jack, I'm not an idiot.

Jack: Thought it was worth a go. I'm hungry.

6

ALL-IN
REST

The main theme today is rest.

[Deep breath in... Hold it... And slowly breathe out.]

Rest is so, so important, and yet it's so often the thing that we don't do when we're busy, because we're busy and we've got so much to do!

It's crucial that we take time to just 'be'. No matter what's going on in our lives, whatever stage of life we're at. We hope that during the service you, and those you are leading, will have at least a little time to be who you / they are and to 'rest' in God's presence.

STORY

So **Jesus and the disciples** went out on the water to get away from the curious crowd who were surrounding them.

Jesus had been healing and teaching people all morning, and He was ready for a rest. So that's exactly what He did; **went for a rest.**

There were still people to heal, there were still things to teach, but He got in a boat and left it all behind... It'll still be there later! He then promptly went to sleep... then the storm happened, and you know the rest of the story I think...

The important thing here, for this service, is that Jesus took time out to rest.

IDEAS

Facilities for resting are important.

If you have uncomfortable chairs in your church, perhaps **provide cushions** for people. If you have carpet, you could invite people to **take their shoes off** if it makes them more comfortable.

Think **over-the-top comfort.** Let's help people rest!

ORDER OF SERVICE

3 MINS — **INTRODUCTION / WELCOME**

3 MINS — **SING** *Everybody's Welcome*

2 MINS — **PRAY** Psalm 100 *(The Message)*

4 MINS — **SING** *Let Everything That Has Breath* — **CREATE** PRAISE prayers

3 MINS — **CREATE** STOP sign

10 MINS — **ACT** *Jesus calms the storm*
SCRIPT *see page 100*

2 MINS — **TELL 1** Even Jesus rested
SCRIPT *see page 97*

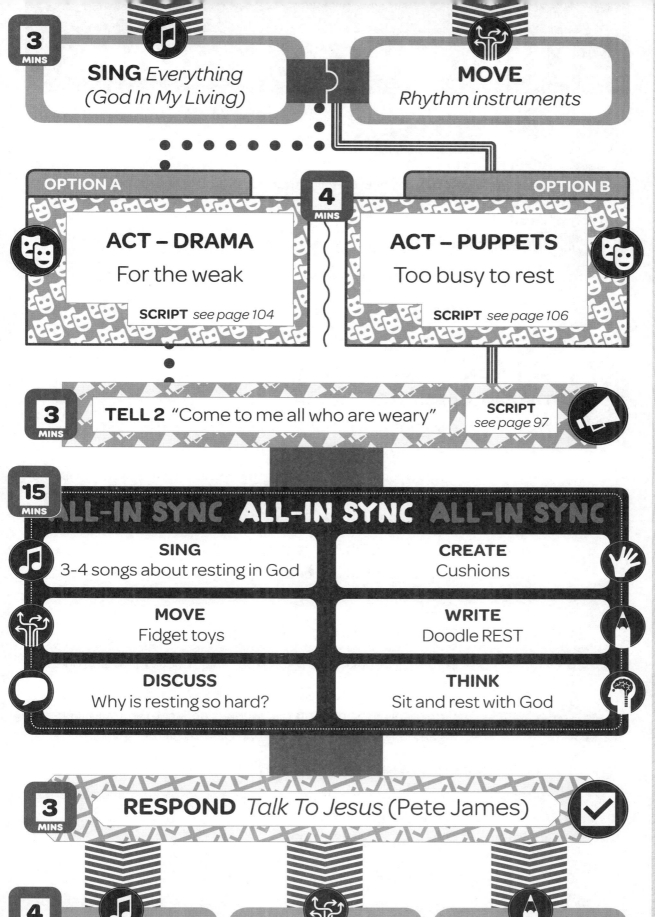

3 MINS — **SING** *Everything (God In My Living)* 🎵

MOVE Rhythm instruments

4 MINS

OPTION A

ACT – DRAMA

For the weak

SCRIPT *see page 104*

OPTION B

ACT – PUPPETS

Too busy to rest

SCRIPT *see page 106*

3 MINS — **TELL 2** "Come to me all who are weary"   **SCRIPT** *see page 97*

15 MINS — ALL-IN SYNC ALL-IN SYNC ALL-IN SYNC

🎵 **SING** 3-4 songs about resting in God	**CREATE** Cushions 🖐
↝ **MOVE** Fidget toys	**WRITE** Doodle REST ✏
💬 **DISCUSS** Why is resting so hard?	**THINK** Sit and rest with God 🧠

3 MINS — **RESPOND** *Talk To Jesus* (Pete James) ✅

4 MINS

SING 🎵
Yesterday, Today and Forever

MOVE ↝
Actions on chorus

WRITE 🔥
"What is God like?" wall

THE FINER DETAIL

SING ▶ CREATE

SING

Lead the congregation in *Let Everything That Has Breath***.

CREATE

Make a giant word PRAISE on a large piece of paper on the floor.

Provide felt-tip pens and ask people to draw pictures to praise God or write praise prayers.

CREATE ◉ STOP SIGN

The Easy Option STOP coaster!

You need: Squares of card – one for each person
Pens

Get everyone to write STOP on their square of card, and perhaps draw a border around the edge to make it look a bit like a road-sign. Easy!

The Medium Option STOP on a stick

You need: Strips of paper (which become square when folded) – one per person
Lollipop sticks – one per person
Pens
Double-sided sticky tape

Before giving out the strips of paper, stick a piece of tape on one side.

Invite people to fold their strip over the top of their lollipop stick (after peeling the back off the double-sided tape) and stick it all together. They should then write STOP on their mini-sign.

The Tricky Option Shaped stop sign

You need: Strips of paper (which become square when folded) – one per person
Lollipop sticks – one per person
Pens
Scissors
Double-sided sticky tape

Get people to make their basic stop sign (as in The Medium Option), then they can use the scissors to shape the STOP sign into a hexagon shape.

 See *www.bigministries.co.uk/theallinthing* for tips and help.

* Copyright details for songs can be found on page 108.

TELL 1 ⦿ EVEN JESUS RESTED

Jesus and His disciples had had a busy day. They had been surrounded by people. Jesus had been healing people left, right and centre and had been teaching. He must have been worn out... So He went for a rest.

Jesus knew there would still be people to heal, Jesus knew there was still things to share with the crowd. However, He got in his boat and left it all behind.

There will always be stuff to do. Like Jesus, we need to learn to just leave it and go and rest when we need it.

I love it that Jesus had just fallen asleep and there was a massive storm. It's as if He then tells the storm to chill out a bit, too!

Rest is important. Even Jesus rested.

 Teach the congregation the phrase **"even Jesus rested"** and some physical signs. See *www.bigministries.co.uk/theallinthing* for details.

SING ▶ MOVE

SING

Lead the congregation in singing *Everything (God In My Living)***.

MOVE

Provide some rhythm instruments – drums and shakers – for this song.

Teach people a couple of simple rhythms to play along with the song (see *www.bigministries.co.uk/theallinthing* if you need some ideas). Continue to lead them through the song so it doesn't descend into rhythm instrument chaos! (Collect them in after the song too.)

TELL 2 ⦿ "COME TO ME ALL WHO ARE WEARY"

Jesus, in Matthew 11:28, says: *"Come to me all who are weary, and I will give you rest."*

Jesus, as we have already thought about, knew how to rest. I guess, in many ways, He learnt from God the Father, who in the act of creation took a day off to rest too.

He promises that if we come to Him, He will give us rest.

But we have to come to Him... We have to take a break... We have to spend time doing absolutely nothing, with Him.

You never know, He might say something new to you, or tell you something you needed to hear... But unless we STOP *[hold up STOP sign]*, His message might not get through.

SING

Sing a few songs about resting in God's presence.

I Will Say Lou Fellingham, Nathan Fellingham, Busbee

Here I Am To Worship (Light Of The World) Tim Hughes

What A Faithful God Dawn Critchley, Robert Critchley

In Your Way Graham Kendrick

Like A River Glorious Frances R. Havergal

Everything Will Be Alright Damian Herbert

There Is A Place Of Quiet Rest Cleland B. McAfee

To Be In Your Presence Noel Richards

Our Confidence Is In The Lord Noel Richards

Copyright details for these songs can be found on page 108.

CREATE • Cushions

You will need:

- ◉ Cheap IKEA cushions
- ◉ Fabric paints

Invite the people in the **CREATE** zone to make a cushion to remind them how important resting with God is. They could perhaps decorate it with some Bible verses or patterns that are soothing (!). They could even turn it into a STOP sign like their mini sign they made earlier.

An easier alternative for the **CREATE** zone is to put out a load of craft materials and allow people to interpret REST as they rest! Paper, pens, glue, stickers, stick on shapes, tissue paper... anything you have, really!

MOVE • Fidget Toys

You will need:

- ◉ A load of fidget toys

The Movers in your congregation will probably be the ones who find resting the hardest, but it's something that we need to practice.

Provide a lot of fidget toys (tangle toys and squiggly things, stress balls and the like). If you haven't got these, beanbags or pipe cleaners are pretty good!

Challenge the Movers to just sit... and listen to God; rest in His presence.

WRITE

Make sure you have some nice writing paper, nice pens and Bibles available.

To try and relax the Writers' brains too, challenge them to just doodle with the word REST. Perhaps writing it in different ways and languages if they know them. Doodling and listening to God.

DISCUSS

Someone leading the discussion is ideal.

Do you rest enough?

What do you need to do to rest? How often do you do this?

Why do we feel the need to be busy the whole time?

Why do we feel guilty when we do nothing?

How much do you think God wants us to rest?

THINK

Make available: Bibles, cushions, ear defenders, paper, pens and even mp3 players with headphones.

The thinkers are probably going to love just 'being' with God... But the questions are available if they need something specific to think about.

Do you rest enough?

What do you need to do to rest? How often do you do this?

Why do we feel the need to be busy the whole time?

Why do we feel guilty when we do nothing?

How much do you think God wants us to rest?

RESPOND

Invite everyone to sit. Play *Talk to Jesus** over people. This song is on *The All-In Thing Songs* CD.

SING MOVE WRITE

SING

*Yesterday, Today and Forever**.

MOVE

 Signs on the chorus – see *www.bigministries.co.uk/theallinthing*.

WRITE

Provide space for people to write words or draw pictures of what God is like.

It's good to be reminded of who God is, and in whom we are resting!

PRAY

It's not on the order of service, but do close the service with prayer!

ACT ● STORY

JESUS CALMS THE STORM ● MATTHEW 8: 23-27

This is a multiple choice story. *Every so often, the audience will be given three options of what could have happened in the story. They must then signify which answer they think is right. This might work best if you split the audience in to two teams, to add an element of competition, and judge each answer by the majority of votes from each team. For the audience to vote you could provide each person with three different coloured cards, or ask them to stand up for one answer, put their hands on their head for another, and put their hands in the air for another. It's up to you how you do it... just don't expect everyone to give you the most sensible answer.*

Characters:
- Jesus
- Disciple 1
- Disciple 2
- Batman

You will need:
- A set of three different coloured cards (enough for everyone in the audience)
- A boat
- A huge fish
- Some silly dressing-up items
- Water pistol
- Paper cut out of the 'Superman' logo

Before you start the story, teach the audience how to use the **coloured cards** *for choosing an answer.*

[Enter stage – Disciples 1 and 2 in a boat]

Narrator 1: Night time was closing in and Jesus and His disciples had decided to do something. But what had they decided to do?

Narrator 2: Had they decided to go to Alton Towers?

Disciple 1: Let's all go to Alton Towers for Jesus' birthday. We'll really surprise Him!

Disciple 2: YEAH! I love Alton Towers. Especially the log flume... WOOOOO!

Narrator 1: Did they form a boy band?

Disciple 1: Let's form a boy band called 'Take This'.

Disciples 1 and 2: *[Singing to the tune of the Take That song,* Greatest Day*]* Today this could be the greatest fish that we've caught.

Narrator 2: Or did they get in a boat and go to the other side of the Sea of Galilee?

Disciple 1: Let's get into a boat and go to the other side of the Sea of Galilee.

Disciple 2: YEAH! I love boats!

Narrator 1: So, hold up [blue] for, Alton Towers; [orange] for, a boy band; or [green] for, they got in a boat.

Narrator 2: They did, of course, get into a boat and sail across to the other side of the Sea of Galilee.

Disciple 1: Come on fellas, let's get going.

Disciple 2: Hold on. Where's Jesus?

Narrator 1: And where was Jesus?

Narrator 2: Was Jesus walking on water?

Disciple 2: Hold on. Where's Jesus?

Disciple 1: Look! Who's that over there?

[Enter stage – Jesus]

Jesus: It's me – Jesus!

Disciples 1 and 2: WOW! He's walking on water!

[Jesus climbs into boat and lies down]

Narrator 1: Was Jesus sleeping?

Disciple 2: Hold on. Where's Jesus?

Disciple 1: Oh, look. There He is, at the end of the boat. He's sleeping. Let's leave Him alone, He's had a busy day.

Narrator 2: Or was Jesus having fun with the fancy dress box?

[Jesus puts on a wig or a hat or some funny glasses]

Disciple 2: Hold on! Where's Jesus?

Jesus: I'm here! Look, it's me… I'm just having fun with the fancy dress.

Narrator 1: So, hold up [blue] for, Jesus was walking on water; [orange] for, Jesus was sleeping; or [green] for, Jesus was in fancy dress.

Narrator 2: And the correct answer is… Jesus was sleeping. Now, after setting off in their boat, the disciples decided that they would sing a little song, as they were accustomed to doing on their usual boat trips.

Disciples 1 and 2: Row, row, row your boat gently down the stream, merrily, merrily, merrily, merrily, life is but a dream.

Narrator 2: And as they continued to sing…

Disciples 1 and 2: Row, row, row your boat…

Narrator 1: One by one…

Disciples 1 and 2: Gently down the stream...

Narrator 2: They stopped singing...

Disciple 1: Merrily, merrily, merrily... merrily...

Narrator 1: And each of them stared and pointed at something only a short way from the boat.

Disciples 1 and 2: Look... at... that!

Narrator 2: But, what were they staring at? Was it Batman?

Disciples 1 and 2: Look... at... that!

[Enter stage – Batman]

Batman: Dun-ner-dun-ner-dun-ner-dun-ner Batmaaan!

Disciple 2: It's Batman!

[Exit stage – Batman]

Narrator 1: Was it a huge wave?

Disciples 1 and 2: Look... at... that!

Disciple 1: It's... it's... it's... It's a huge wave heading straight for us!

Disciples 1 and 2: *[Holding on tightly to one another]* ARRRRRGHHHH!

Narrator 2: Or was it a dolphin?

Disciples 1 and 2: Look... at... that!

Disciple 2: It's a dolphin.

Disciple 1: Ooh, let's go and say hello.

Narrator 1: So, hold up [blue] for, Batman; [orange] for, a huge wave; or [green] for, a dolphin.

Narrator 2: And the correct answer is... They saw a huge wave.

Disciple 2: Brace yourself! It's gonna hit us!

Disciple 1: Yikes! I'm soaked.

Disciple 2: Look out, here comes another one!

Narrator 1: Wave after wave hit the boat as a storm quickly arose and became more and more ferocious.

[Disciples sway around in the boat]

Narrator 2: The wind blew harder and the rain came down heavier; the boat rocked forwards and backwards and left and right, chucking the disciples all over the place.

Narrator 1: Yet Jesus remained asleep at the end of the boat.

Disciple 1: What do we do!? We're going to drown!

Disciple 2: There's only one thing we can do. What we do is...

Narrator 2: And what did they do? Did they wake up Jesus?

Disciple 2: What we do is... we wake up Jesus.

> One of the narrators could maybe throw a small cup of water in the disciples' faces, or squirt them with a water pistol.

Disciple 1: Good idea. *[Shaking Jesus]* Jesus, wake up!!!

Narrator 1: Did they go surfing?

Disciple 2: What we do is... create some surf boards, dude. Like, out of the boat, and then like, totally surf our way to the shore.

Disciple 1: Far out dude! Kowabunga!

Narrator 2: Or, did they do nothing?

Disciple 2: What we do is... nothing. We're with Jesus. We don't need to panic. He'll sort it out when He's ready.

Narrator 1: So, hold up [blue] for, they woke up Jesus; [orange] for, they went surfing; or [green] for, they did nothing.

Narrator 2: And the correct answer is, they woke up Jesus.

Disciples 1: Jesus, Jesus, wake up! We're going to drown!

[Disciples gripping hold of Jesus in fear]

Disciple 2: Why are you sleeping? What are we going to do. HELP!

Jesus: OK. Calm down... and let go of me. We're not going to drown.

Narrator 1: But what did Jesus do next? Did He turn into Superman?

Jesus: We're not going to drown.

Disciple 1: Why not?

Jesus: *[Revealing the Superman 'S' logo underneath His shirt]* Because I'm Superman! Hold on to me and I'll fly you all out of here!

> Here, you could maybe get hold of the Superman theme tune and play a quick short clip.

Narrator 2: Did He get everyone to kneel and pray?

Jesus: We're not going to drown. Everybody kneel around the edge of the boat and we'll all pray that the storm will stop.

Narrator 1: Or did He speak to the weather?

Jesus: We're not going to drown. Wind, waves, rain... Be still.

Disciple 2: Jesus just spoke to the weather!

Narrator 2: So, hold up [blue] for, Jesus was Superman; [orange] for, they all prayed; or [green] for, Jesus spoke to the weather.

Narrator 1: The correct answer is... Jesus spoke to the weather. He commanded the storm to be still and it was still.

Disciple 1: No way! Did you see that!?

Disciple 2: The storm's stopped. Jesus can even command the weather to do what He wants.

Narrator 2: And after all of that commotion, the disciples and Jesus continued safely on their trip to the other side of the Sea of Galilee.

Jesus and Disciples 1 and 2: Row, row, row your boat gently down the stream, merrily, merrily, merrily, merrily, life is but a dream... *[Singing fades out as the disciples and Jesus exit stage]* Row, row, row your boat...

ACT ● DRAMA

FOR THE WEAK

> **You will need:**
> ◉ A clipboard and pen
> ◉ Two or more helpers to carry Ben at the end of the sketch

[Enter stage – Ben with clipboard]

Ben: So much to do. So very little time. *[Reading clipboard]* Let me see here... 7:31 – make breakfast – done. 7:32 – watch milk turn chocolatey – done. 7:33 – eat breakfast, mmm – done. 7:35 – get dressed – done... Done... Done... Done... Ah, here we are – two minutes to tidy the church. Urgh! Who made this place so untidy? I'll never get it done in just two minutes.

[Enter stage – Jen]

Ben: Something needs to go... Pilates? Maybe. Listening to 1D... Erm, no way!

Jen: Hey everybody. Hello Ben.

Ben: STOP WASTING MY TIME!!!

Jen: Wow! Wasn't that a touch excessive?

Ben: Excessive? Excessive? Jen we have been given just twenty-four hours a day in which we must fit everything. I don't want to waste a single minute and so I have created a minute-by-minute schedule. Engaging in idle chit-chat is not on my schedule. So, no, I do not think that it was excessive. *[Muttering to clipboard]* I guess if I cut out "pleases" and "thank yous" today, I can allow time for this pointless conversation.

Jen: Ben, you seem a little higher maintenance than usual. When was the last time you had rest?

Ben: Rest?

Jen: Yeah, you know. Like, a day off.

Ben: Rest? Day off? Rest is for the weak. I no longer take a day off and in so doing I have increased weekly productivity by an impressive sixteen point six percent.

Jen: But everyone needs to rest, Ben. It helps restore our energy. Why do you think we sleep?

Ben: We don't.

Jen: What do you mean, "we don't"?

Ben: I mean, *you* sleep but *I* don't, because you are weak and I am not. I found that by cutting out sleep each day I have increased daily productivity by an astounding fifty percent.

Jen: Well, if you don't sleep where do you get the energy to do your carefully planned-out schedule? How are you functioning?

Ben: My own special blend of Coco-Pops, fizzy pop and fairly traded coffee, a concoction that I was able to develop due to cutting out rest from my schedule.

Jen: Ben, this is no way to live. When are you going to enjoy life? When will you stop and smell the roses?

Ben: Let me check... *[Reading clipboard]* 4:14 to 4:17 – enjoy life. 5:27 to 5:28 – stop and smell roses. I will be enjoying life at fourteen minutes past four and smelling roses at twenty-seven minutes past five.

Jen: Is that it? Four minutes?

Ben: No, of course not. I will be doing the same tomorrow.

Jen: Ben, you can't go on forever without rest, without stopping. Rest was designed with human beings in mind. We need to rest. Now, don't you think that you should maybe go home and catch up on your beauty sleep? *[Ben closes his eyes and snores]*

Jen: Ben? Ben? Well, I think that just reinforces my point, doesn't it? Not that you're conscious to realise it... *[Ben falls to the floor and continues to sleep]*

Jen: Great! We're going to need to do something about that if we want to finish this service. A little help here please.

[Enter stage – two or more helpers to carry Ben off stage. Exit all]

Ben: *[Talking in sleep]* No, Mummy, I don't want to give my dummy to the Dummy Fairy!

ACT ○ PUPPETS

TOO BUSY TO REST

[Enter – Jack, 'holding' a present]

Jack: Jill, Jill, come here, I've got something to show you.

Jill: *[From off stage]* Hold on Jack, I'm just in the middle of something, I'll be there in a minute

Jack: Aw, OK, I'll wait. Oh hello everyone. Are you OK? I'm OK... I'm excited, because I've made something for Jill. It's a present... It's not her birthday or anything... But I think she's going to like it. I like surprises... *[whistling]* Do do doooo... Where is she? Jill, I thought you were coming here!

Jill: I am, I said I'm in the middle of something... I'm nearly done. Stop talking to me and then I'll be done quicker.

Jack: OK. Wow, she sounds stressed. I wonder if she's OK. *[Awkward pause]* JIIIIIIILLLLLLLLLLL!

Jill: Alright, alright *[out of breath]*, I'm coming. *[Enter – Jill]* Hi. I'm here.

Jack: There you are. Nice to see you.

Jill: *[Rushing]* Yeah, yeah, nice to see you too... What do you want?

Jack: Oh well, I just wondered how you are – how are you?

Jill: Jack, I'm busy.

Jack: Oh.

Jill: I've got so much on at the minute, and now you're bothering me and my to do list is just getting longer and longer and I just haven't got time to stop and I haven't even had breakfast this morning and Jack, do you need me for something or can I go and get on please?

Jack: Well, I guess you could...

Jill: Thanks Jack, I'll see you later. *[Exit – Jill]*

Jack: But I just wanted to give you... Aw... *[Sigh]*

[Enter Alex]

Alex: Hey Jack, you OK?

Jack: Hi Alex, yeah I guess so.

Alex: Is that a present?

Jack: Yep, I made it for Jill, but she's too busy...

Alex: What do you mean?

Jack: Well, I asked her how she was – you know, a bit of chit-chat before I gave her the present and she said she was busy and then went off on one about how much she had to do – then she went!

Alex: Oh dear. Let's see if we can find her.

Jack: OK.

Alex: Jill... Jill... can you come here, please?

Jill: NOW What? *[Enter – Jill]* I told you I'm busy...

Alex: Hello Jill, what's going on? Are you OK?

Jill: No, I'm not OK, Alex, I'm busy.

Alex: Oh, well what are you busy with?

Jill: EVERYTHING, I have a to-do list as long as my leg *[head on one side]*...

Jack: Told you.

Alex: Right, well when was the last time you had a rest, Jill?

Jill: REST? I don't even know what that is.

Alex: Jill, resting is really important. There are always things to do, there's always a to do list... but if you don't rest, you'll make yourself ill... and you'll end up not seeing your friends.

Jill: I know, but...

Alex: Even God rested, Jill...

Jill: What?

Alex: God made the world in six days, and then on the seventh day, He rested.

Jill: Oh.

Jack: AND if you'd stopped for a second you would have seen that I made you a present... it's here... if you want it.

Jill: Oh Jack, I'm sorry. I'd love my present.

Jack: It's popcorn... I made it... It's got caramel sauce on... I've got a film ready too for us to watch while we eat it.

Jill: But I've got too much to...

Alex: Jill, think... what's important?

Jill: OK. Jack, that'd be nice.

Alex: Off you go then, you two.

Jack: Come on, Jill!

[Exit – Jack, Jill and Alex]

SONG INFORMATION FOR SECTIONS 4-7

4 JESUS IS ALIVE

Resurrection Hymn (See What A Morning) Keith Getty / Stuart Townend • © 2003 Thankyou Music (Adm. by CapitolCMGPublishing.com excl. UK & Europe, adm. by Integrity Music, part of the David C Cook family, songs@integritymusic.com) CCLI# 4108797

He's My Saviour Joel Payne • © Joel Payne – Resoundworship.org (Admin. by The Jubilate Group) CCLI# 5314920

Hero Of The World Damian Herbert • © Song Solutions Daybreak (Admin. by Song Solutions www.songsolutions.org) CCLI# 6493967

Come People Of The Risen King Keith & Kristyn Getty / Stuart Townend • © 2007 Thankyou Music (Adm. by CapitolCMGPublishing.com excl. UK & Europe, adm. by Integrity Music, part of the David C Cook family, songs@integritymusic.com) CCLI# 5232617

For This Purpose Graham Kendrick • © 1985 Thankyou Music (Adm. by CapitolCMGPublishing.com excl. UK & Europe, adm. by Integrity Music, part of the David C Cook family, songs@integritymusic.com) CCLI# 24126

He Has Risen Gerald Coates / Noel Richards / Tricia Richards • © 1993 Thankyou Music (Adm. by CapitolCMGPublishing.com excl. UK & Europe, adm. by Integrity Music, part of the David C Cook family, songs@integritymusic.com) CCLI# 1045252

Glorious Day (Living He Loved Me) John Wilbur Chapman / Mark Hall / Michael Bleecker • © 2009 Word Music, LLC (Admin by Small Stone Media) / My Refuge Music (Admin by Song Solutions www.songsolutions.org) : Sony/ATV Tree Publishing (Admin. by Sony/ATV Music Publishing) CCLI# 5638022

5 THE HOLY SPIRIT'S POWER

Come You Thankful People Sam Hargreaves • © Sam Hargreaves – RESOUNDworship.org (Admin. by The Jubilate Group) CCLI# 5464155

Show Your Power (He Is The Lord) Kevin Prosch • © 1991 Mercy/Vineyard Publishing (Admin by Vineyard Music USA) (Adm. Song Solutions www.songsolutions.org) CCLI# 861891

I Believe Damian Herbert • © Song Solutions Daybreak (Admin. by Song Solutions www.songsolutions.org) CCLI# 6493974

Spirit Break Out Ben Bryant / Myles Dhillon / Luke Hellbronth / Tim Hughes • © 2010 Thankyou Music (Adm. by CapitolCMGPublishing.com excl. UK & Europe, adm. by Integrity Music, part of the David C Cook family, songs@integritymusic.com) CCLI# 6058450

Open The Eyes Of My Heart Paul Baloche • © 1997 Integrity's Hosanna! Music (Adm. by CapitolCMGPublishing.com excl. UK & Europe, adm. by Integrity Music, part of the David C Cook family, songs@integritymusic.com) CCLI# 2298355

Consuming Fire Tim Hughes • © 2002 Thankyou Music (Adm. by CapitolCMGPublishing.com excl. UK & Europe, adm. by Integrity Music, part of the David C Cook family, songs@integritymusic.com) CCLI# 3818569

Holy Spirit We Welcome You Chris Bowater • © 1986 Sovereign Lifestyle Music CCLI# 215942

Spirit Of The Living God Daniel Iverson • © 1935, Renewed 1963 Birdwing Music (Admin. by Song Solutions www.songsolutions.org) CCLI# 23488

6 REST

Let Everything That Has Breath Matt Redman • © 1997 Thankyou Music (Adm. by CapitolCMGPublishing.com excl. UK & Europe, adm. by Integrity Music, part of the David C Cook family, songs@integritymusic.com) CCLI# 2430979

God In My Living Tim Hughes • © 2005 Thankyou Music (Adm. by CapitolCMGPublishing.com excl. UK & Europe, adm. by Integrity Music, part of the David C Cook family, songs@integritymusic.com) CCLI# 4685258

Talk To Jesus Pete James • © 2014 Elevation www.songsolutions.org CCLI# 7012857

Yesterday, Today And Forever Vicky Beeching • © 2002 Thankyou Music (Adm. by CapitolCMGPublishing.com excl. UK & Europe, adm. by Integrity Music, part of the David C Cook family, songs@integritymusic.com) CCLI# 3994706

You Give Rest Lou Fellingham / Nathan Fellingham / Busbee • © 2005 Thankyou Music / The Livingstone Collective (Adm. by CapitolCMGPublishing.com excl. UK & Europe, adm. by Integrity Music, part of the David C Cook family, songs@integritymusic.com) CCLI# 4814328

What A Faithful God Dawn Critchley / Robert Critchley • © 1989 Thankyou Music (Adm. by CapitolCMGPublishing.com excl. UK & Europe, adm. by Integrity Music, part of the David C Cook family, songs@integritymusic.com) CCLI# 605095

In Your Way Graham Kendrick • © 1976 Make Way Music www.grahamkendrick.co.uk CCLI# 648746

Everything Will Be Alright Damian Herbert • © 2008 Song Solutions Daybreak (Admin. by Song Solutions www.songsolutions.org) CCLI# 5344945

Like A River Glorious Frances R Havergal • Public Domain CCLI# 2648510

Near To The Heart Of God Cleland Boyd McAfee • Pubilc Domain

To Be In Your Presence Noel Richards • © 1991 Thankyou Music (Adm. by CapitolCMGPublishing.com excl. UK & Europe, adm. by Integrity Music, part of the David C Cook family, songs@integritymusic.com) CCLI# 918122

Our Confidence Is In The Lord Noel & Tricia Richards • © 1989 Thankyou Music (Adm. by CapitolCMGPublishing.com excl. UK & Europe, adm. by Integrity Music, part of the David C Cook family, songs@integritymusic.com) CCLI# 649642

7 GOD IS WITH US

Hallelujah (Your Love Is Amazing) Brenton Brown / Brian Doerksen • © 2000 Vineyard Songs (UK/Eire) (Admin. by Vineyard Music UK) (Adm. Song Solutions www.songsolutions.org CCLI# 3091812

You Never Let Go Matt & Beth Redman • © 2005 Thankyou Music (Adm. by CapitolCMGPublishing.com excl. UK & Europe, adm. by Integrity Music, part of the David C Cook family, songs@integritymusic.com) CCLI# 4674166

Unchanging (Great Is Your Faithfulness) Chris Tomlin • © 2002 sixsteps Music / worshiptogether.com songs (Adm. by CapitolCMGPublishing.com excl. UK & Europe, adm. by Integrity Music, part of the David C Cook family, songs@integritymusic.com) CCLI# 4016669

Be Bold, Be Strong Morris Chapman • © 1984 Word Music, LLC (Admin. by Small Stone Media) (Adm. Song Solutions www.songsolutions.org) CCLI# 58563

Be Still David J Evans • © 1986 Thankyou Music (Adm. by CapitolCMGPublishing.com excl. UK & Europe, adm. by Integrity Music, part of the David C Cook family, songs@integritymusic.com) CCLI# 120824

For This I Have Jesus (For The Joys And For The Sorrows) Graham Kendrick • © 1994 Make Way Music www.grahamkendrick.co.uk CCLI# 1081278

God Is Able Ben Fielding / Reuben Morgan • © 2010 Hillsong Music Publishing (Admin. by HMTR Limited) CCLI# 5894275

Never Once Jason Ingram / Matt Redman / Tim Wanstall • © 2011 Chrysalis Music Ltd (Admin. by BMG Chrysalis) : Said And Done Music / sixsteps Music / Thankyou Music / worshiptogether.com songs (Adm. by CapitolCMGPublishing.com excl. UK & Europe, adm. by Integrity Music, part of the David C Cook family, songs@integritymusic.com) : Sony/ATV Timber Publishing / West Main Music / Windsor Hill Music (Admin. by Sony/ATV Music Publishing) CCLI# 5997055

The **ALL-IN** Thing

GOD IS WITH US

7

THEME

The main theme today is **God is always with us.**

This is one of those themes that feels a bit obvious. However, it is important for us to go over because **God really is ALWAYS with us**, looking out for us. I think sometimes we can feel as though God is just watching us from a cloud in the sky or something, and that all He's doing is watching and waiting until we slip up. It really isn't like that. God is absolutely going through everything with us, and wants to help us to try and stop making mistakes... If only we paid better attention.

STORY

Jonah was such a cheeky character; I guess the way he behaves resonates a little! I love it...

God gives him a really clear message: "Go to Nineveh". Jonah is all like, "yeah, yeah, I'm going", and then thinks that he can trick God and run away in the opposite direction, as if God isn't already aware of what's happening! So often we do things just like that!

This is such a great story showing God's **compassion, forgiveness** and **sense of humour.** (Surely getting swallowed by a giant fish wasn't a necessary way to save Jonah! Good way to teach him a lesson though, I think!)

IDEAS

You could plan for this service to be in **September**, when a lot of people may have new beginnings, as the new academic year starts.

It's a great way to remind people that God is with them whatever is going on, and wherever they may find themselves.

ORDER OF SERVICE

3 MINS — **INTRODUCTION / WELCOME**

3 MINS — **SING** *Everybody's Welcome*

2 MINS — **PRAY** Psalm 117 *(The Message)*

3 MINS
- **SING** *Hallelujah (Your Love Is Amazing)*
- **CREATE** Play-dough

3 MINS — **CREATE** Fish

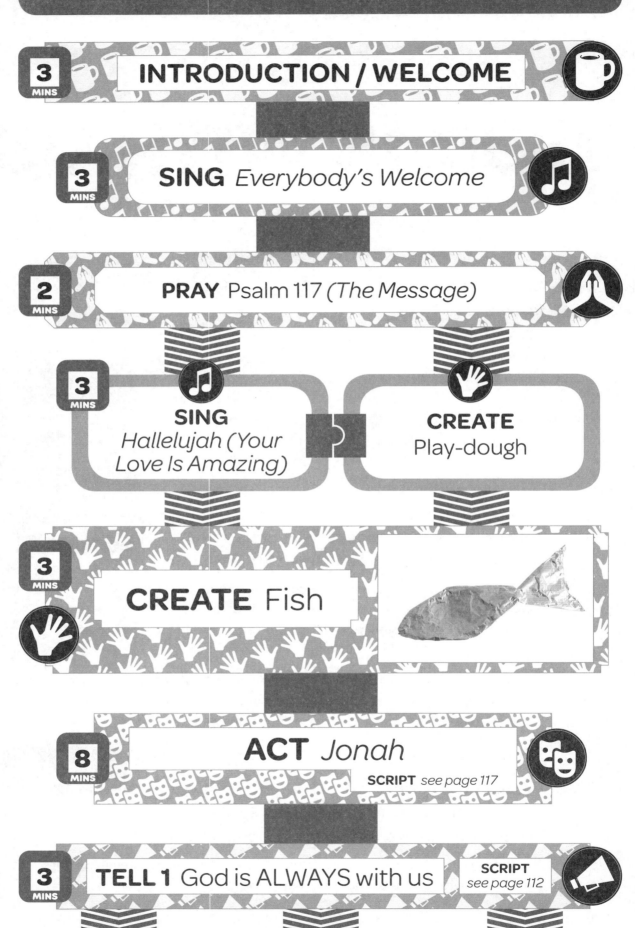

8 MINS — **ACT** *Jonah*
SCRIPT *see page 117*

3 MINS — **TELL 1** God is ALWAYS with us
SCRIPT *see page 112*

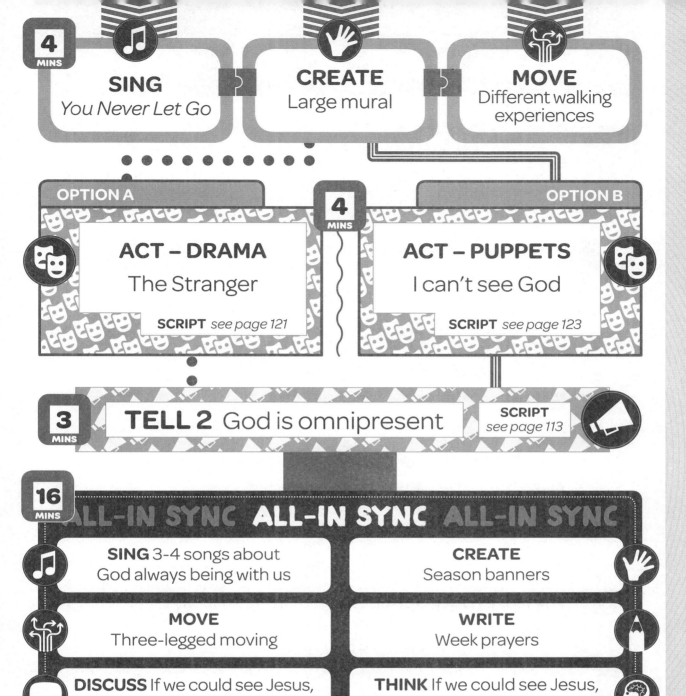

4 MINS

SING *You Never Let Go*

CREATE Large mural

MOVE Different walking experiences

OPTION A

4 MINS

ACT – DRAMA The Stranger

SCRIPT *see page 121*

OPTION B

ACT – PUPPETS I can't see God

SCRIPT *see page 123*

3 MINS

TELL 2 God is omnipresent

SCRIPT *see page 113*

16 MINS

ALL-IN SYNC ALL-IN SYNC ALL-IN SYNC

SING 3-4 songs about God always being with us

CREATE Season banners

MOVE Three-legged moving

WRITE Week prayers

DISCUSS If we could see Jesus, what difference would it make?

THINK If we could see Jesus, what difference would it make?

3 MINS

RESPOND We will trust God. Make a giant fish

4 MINS

SING *Unchanging (Great Is Your Faithfulness)*

MOVE Sign language

THINK How does God show His faithfulness?

THE FINER DETAIL

SING ▸ CREATE

SING

Lead the congregation in *Hallelujah (Your Love Is Amazing)***.**

CREATE

Provide an area with plastic sheeting on the floor and lots of play-dough. Invite those who would like to, to create something to worship God, to make an offering to Him.

CREATE ◉ FISH

The Easy Option Pipe cleaner fish

You need: Pipe cleaners – one per person

Lead everyone in making a simple fish shape with their pipe cleaner.

The Slightly Trickier Option Pipe cleaner, foil fish

You need: Pipe cleaners – one per person
Pieces of foil – one per person

Lead everyone in making a simple fish shape with their pipe cleaner.

Then use the foil to 'coat' the whole of the fish to make it shiny!

The Most Tricky Option Pipe cleaner, foil fish with scales!

You need: Pipe cleaners – one per person
Pieces of foil – one per person
Pens with lids on

Lead everyone in making a simple fish shape with their pipe cleaner.

Then use the foil to 'coat' the whole of the fish to make it shiny!

Use the lidded pen to mark scales on the foil. The tricky part is not pressing too hard, as you may then make a hole in the foil!

See *www.bigministries.co.uk/theallinthing* for tips and help.

TELL 1 ◉ GOD IS ALWAYS WITH US

God asked Jonah to do something that was actually quite big and scary. The people of Nineveh were known to be fairly mean and not very tolerant of people telling them what to do. Jonah thought that he would get away with it and could just go somewhere else. He was wrong. Even though it was a scary place, God had promised to be with Jonah. Even though Jonah was afraid, he should have known that God was with him.

Copyright details for songs can be found on page 108.

God was with Jonah even though he went the wrong way. God looked after Jonah even though he completely disobeyed Him. God protected Jonah even when he lied. God listened to Jonah's prayers even when he was stuck inside a fish.

Teach people the phrase: **God is always with us.**

 See *www.bigministries.co.uk/theallinthing* for physical signs to teach the congregation.

SING ◧ CREATE ◧ MOVE

SING

Lead the congregation in singing *You Never Let Go**.

CREATE

Provide a large piece of paper, and paints or pens. You could even find someone before the service to draw the outline of a scene (cityscape if you live in a city, landscape if you live in the country) for people to fill in during this song (and at other points during the service).

MOVE

Provide some different trays of materials for people to walk through – to symbolise the different sorts of experiences we may go through in life – and that God is with us in all of them.

You could have things like mud, water, bark, cornflour and water (this is a very strange sensation!), sand, torn up newspaper and anything else you can think of.

It's probably a good idea to do this on a tarpaulin and with plenty of soapy water and towels for at the end.

Ask people to write a reflection on a piece of paper about the different experiences.

TELL 2 ◉ GOD IS OMNIPRESENT

God is omnipresent. Invite your congregation to say that with you.
God is omnipresent.

This is just a short way of saying that God is always everywhere, all at the same time!

It's easy for us to make God into a bit of a super-human, when actually He is much, much more than that. He is far bigger, and way more incomprehensible.

So much so, that we have a word that can only be used to describe God – omnipresent. God is always right here with me, and He's always right there with you, and there's no logic to that. God is just God!

Let's learn: **God is omnipresent.** Which means God is always everywhere.

 See *www.bigministries.co.uk/theallinthing* for physical signs to teach the congregation to help them remember.

THE FINER DETAIL GOD IS WITH US

SING

Sing a few songs about God being with us at all times.

Be Bold, Be Strong Morris Chapman

10,000 Reasons (Bless The Lord)
Jonas Myrin, Matt Redman

For This I Have Jesus (For The Joys And For The Sorrows) Graham Kendrick

Forever (Give Thanks To The Lord)
Chris Tomlin

Be Still David J. Evans

God Is Able
Ben Fielding, Reuben Morgan

Never Once Jason Ingram,
Matt Redman, Tim Wanstall

Copyright details for these songs can be found on page 108.

CREATE • Season banners

You will need:

- ◉ Squares of fabric
- ◉ Scraps of fabric / felt
- ◉ Glue
- ◉ Permanent marker pens
- ◉ Scissors

In the **CREATE** zone, invite people to create a square which tells a bit of a story about their life at the minute. It could be an abstract picture, it could be a pattern that represents something, or it could be a more classic 'scene' of something significant that's happening in their life at the moment.

Then the idea will be to join them all together to create a banner of seasons – showing something of where we are at as a church.

When people have completed their 'tile', perhaps have them cut out one of the letters of GOD IS WITH US and then when the banner is made, this can be stuck on it too.

MOVE • Three-legged moving

You will need:

- ◉ Scarves
- ◉ Obstacles

Create a relatively easy obstacle course (with chairs to go around, for example).

Create three-legged people by tying two legs (from different people) together, and get them to walk the course.

Talk about:

How does it feel to have someone stuck with you all the time?

Is it different to how we feel with God being with us?

WRITE

Make sure you have some nice writing paper, nice pens and Bibles available.

Week Prayers:

"On Monday when_____, God you are with me.", etc.

Use the title **Week Prayers** as your starter. Go through the week and declare, by writing it down, that God is with you in everything you do.

DISCUSS

Someone leading the discussion is ideal.

If Jesus were physically walking next to you, what difference would it make to how you live?

Why may it not make so much difference when we can't see Jesus?

How can we truly live like God is with us at all times?

THINK

Make available: Bibles, cushions, ear defenders, paper, pens and even mp3 players with headphones.

If Jesus were physically walking next to you, what difference would it make to how you live?

Why may it not make so much difference when we can't see Jesus?

Spend some time reflecting on St. Patrick's *Breastplate Prayer:*

Christ be with me, Christ within me,

Christ behind me, Christ before me,

Christ beside me, Christ to win me,

Christ to comfort and restore me.

Christ beneath me, Christ above me,

Christ in quiet, Christ in danger,

Christ in hearts of all that love me,

Christ in mouth of friend and stranger.

RESPOND

Listen to *You Need Not Fear** – this song is on *The All-In Thing Songs* CD.

 You could also lead the sign language for this song.
See *www.bigministries.co.uk/theallinthing* for the signs.

Create a giant fish outline on the floor (perhaps using masking tape).

Invite people, as they listen to the song, to bring the fish that they have made to the big fish and overlay them to create the scales for the fish. As they bring the fish, they are using this as a sign that they are going to trust God no matter what He asks us to do, knowing that He will be with us.

SING ▶ MOVE ▶ THINK

SING

Unchanging (Great Is Your Faithfulness)*.

MOVE

 Sign language for parts of the song –
see *www.bigministries.co.uk/theallinthing* for details and ideas.

THINK

Invite those who like to think, to spend a bit of time reflecting on Psalm 25:10.

> *The Lord leads with unfailing love and faithfulness all
> who keep His covenant and obey His demands.*

You may also want to think about "how does God show unfailing faithfulness?"

PRAY

It's not on the order of service, but do close the service with prayer!

ACT ● STORY

JONAH ● THE BOOK OF JONAH

Characters:
- Narrator 1
- Narrator 2
- Jonah
- Sailor 1
- Sailor 2
- Sailor 3
- A few people dressed as the Giant Fish

You will need:
- A boat
- Water pistols

Teach the audience these trigger words *before reading the story*:

Boat　*Say* **"ahoy there!"**

Shore　*Say* **"she sells sea shells on the sea shore"** *as fast as you can.*

Storm　*Say* **"BANG! CRASH!"** *and clap your hands once if you're able to.*

[Enter stage – Jonah and the sailors, all in a boat]

Narrator 1: Jonah had hopped aboard a **boat**; a **boat** headed for a place called, Tarshish.

Narrator 2: After setting sail, Jonah, along with the other sailors, was in the middle of the vast sea, far from **shore.**

Sailors 1, 2 and 3: *[Singing]* Oh, what shall we do with a drunken sailor, what shall we do with a drunken sailor, what shall we do with a drunken sailor, early in the morning!?

Sailor 1: Sssh. How inappropriate. Don't tell anyone you're drunk.

Sailor 2: I'm not drunk.

Sailor 3: I'm not drunk either.

Sailor 1: Oh, erm… Nor am I… That would be wrong at such an hour. *[Sailor 1 then raises his eyebrows and hiccups]*

Narrator 1: Jonah was on his way to Tarshish because it was in the opposite direction to a place called, Nineveh.

Narrator 2: And why is it that you want to go in the opposite direction to Nineveh, Jonah?

Jonah: Sssh. Shut up, will you!? It's none of your business.

Narrator 1: If you don't tell everyone then I will.

> You could have a sign on stage, a bit like a road sign, with two arrows pointing opposite ways: one saying *Tarshish* and one saying *Nineveh.*

Jonah: I'm... going on holiday. That's right. Holiday.

[Jonah lies down in the boat and goes to sleep]

Narrator 1: The real reason that Jonah was heading in the opposite direction to Nineveh was because...

Sailors 1, 2 and 3: *[Interrupting and pointing into the distance]* Look out! **STORRRRRM!**

Narrator 2: But before Narrator 1 could give an explanation as to Jonah's sudden interest in Tarshish, the **boat** carrying Jonah, and several other crew members, was hit by a ferocious **storm**!

Sailors 1, 2 and 3: Arrrrrrrgh!!

Narrator 1: The sailors feared for their lives as the **boat** was tossed forwards and backwards, and left to right, upside down, and back again.

*[Every time the word **wave** is mentioned, the sailors get squirted with a water pistol by a couple of people crouching either side of stage]*

Narrator 2: Wave after **wave** after **wave** after **wave**...

Narrator 1: ... After **wave** after **wave** after **wave**...

Narrator 2: ... After **wave**...

Narrator 1: ... After **wave**... crashed over the side of the **boat**.

Narrator 2: The sailors all cried out for help from the different gods that they worshipped.

Sailors 1, 2 and 3: HELP!

Narrator 1: But no help came.

Narrator 2: Then, they had a brain **wave**. *[Don't forget, **wave** means squirt the sailors!]*

Sailors 1, 2 and 3: Jonah!

Narrator 2: And where was Jonah while all this was going on?

Narrator 1: Jonah was below deck, sleeping.

Sailor 1: Jonah! Wake up!

Sailor 2: How can you sleep through this?

Sailor 3: We're going to drown! Pray to your God to save us!

[Jonah stands to his feet]

Narrator 2: After some strange kind of mystic game, the sailors realised who was to blame for this magnificent **storm** that was bringing them all to the brink of death.

Sailors 1, 2 and 3: Jonah!

Sailor 1: Who are you!?

> Here you could attach some long strips of material to a powerful fan. When you switch the fan on, the bits of material being blown will give the impression of a strong wind.

Sailor 2: Where are you from!?

Sailor 3: What have you done!?

Jonah: Fine! You want to know the truth?

Sailors 1, 2 and 3: YES!

Jonah: You want to know why I'm here?

Sailors 1, 2 and 3: YES!

Jonah: You want to know why this is happening?

Sailors 1, 2 and 3: YES! Tell us.

Jonah: God told me to go to the City of Nineveh because the people there are wicked and evil. God told me to go to the City of Nineveh to show them the right way to live.

Sailor 1: So!? Why didn't you go!?

Jonah: Because... I dislike the people of Nineveh. A lot.

Narrator 1: It was because of Jonah that they were all caught in the middle of a **storm**. It didn't look like God was going to let Jonah run away from this one.

Sailor 2: What do we do then?

Sailor 3: How do we stop the **storm** and all of these **waves**?! *[Squirt with water pistols]*

Sailors 1 and 2: Don't say **'waves'**! *[Water pistols... again!]*

Jonah: Throw me overboard. That is the only thing that will end this **storm**.

Narrator 2: But the sailors did not want to throw Jonah overboard. They didn't want to harm anyone.

Narrator 1: They tried their best to row back to **shore**, but the **storm** was too much and was increasing in ferocity by the minute.

Narrator 2: Eventually, there was nothing else that the sailors could do other than throw Jonah into the sea.

[Sailors pick Jonah up, throw him overboard and, along with the boat, exit stage]

Narrator 1: The **boat** sailed on and the **storm** ended.

Narrator 2: Jonah was left bobbing about in the water wondering what was going to happen to him next.

Jonah: What am I going to do now? I'm not the best swimmer. I can't swim back to **shore**. I'd be better off if a huge fish just swam up to me and ate me.

[Enter stage – Giant Fish]

Narrator 1: Funny you should say that. Just then, a huge fish swam up to Jonah and ate him.

> The Giant Fish could be as simple as having a few people stand in a line with hands on each others shoulders, and the front person doing breast stroke. When Jonah gets swallowed he stands in the middle of the line of people.

Narrator 2: It didn't chew him up as such, but swallowed him whole, meaning Jonah was sat in the smelly belly of a giant fish.

Jonah: Yuck! I hate fish!

Narrator 1: After three days and three nights inside the fish, God commanded the huge sea creature to spew Jonah up onto the **shore**.

Jonah: About time. Fish stink!

Giant Fish: Well, as a matter of fact, I'm not too keen on humans! So there!

[Exit stage – Giant Fish]

Narrator 2: God then spoke to Jonah a second time telling him to go to the City of Nineveh to tell them to turn from their evil ways.

Narrator 1: Which this time, Jonah did.

Narrator 2: And did they turn from their evil ways?

Jonah: Yes, they did.

Narrator 1: Right, who's for fish and chips?

Jonah: That isn't funny.

ACT ● DRAMA

THE STRANGER

[Enter stage – Jen]

Jen: Hello Ben, what are you up... Oh, he's not here. That's weird...

[Enter stage – Ben, who runs across stage]

Ben: Aaaaaaaaaaaargh!

[Exit stage – Ben on other side of stage]

Jen: That's also weird! Ben?

[Enter stage – Ben who runs across stage]

Ben: Aaaaaaaaaaaargh!

Jen: Ben, wait...

[Exit Ben on other side of stage]

Jen: Ben is normally quite strange but this is a little off, even for him. I'll see if I can get him to stop if he does it again.

[Enter stage – Ben who runs across stage]

Ben: Aaaaaaaaaaaargh!

Jen: Ben, stop. One Direction are here.

Ben: Aaaa... One Direction? Where?

Jen: Ah, they just left. You just missed them. Sorry.

Ben: Ah, again? Oh well, where was I? Oh yes, aaaaaaa...

Jen: *[Stopping Ben from running off]* Hang on a minute, Ben. Just calm down. Now, what's the problem? Why are you running around screaming?

Ben: I'm trying to get rid of 'him'.

Jen: 'Him'?

Ben: Yes, 'him'. The one who has been following me everywhere.

Jen: *[Looking offstage]* I can't see anyone. When do you think he started following you?

Ben: Well, it all started this morning when I opened my bedroom curtains to let in the sun. I turned around and there he was, right behind me.

Jen: Really? Who was he?

Ben: Jen, please try not to interrupt.

Jen: Sorry.

Ben: I thought it was strange that he was there but I tried to be polite. I said "hello" and I invited him to join me downstairs for breakfast.

Jen: What did he say?

Ben: Nothing! So, I went downstairs anyway and he came with me but he didn't eat anything. He was just there with me as I ate my Shreddies.

Jen: That's unusual.

Ben: I know, right? Normally, I have Coco-Pops but my sister must have finished them. Anyway, after breakfast I thought I would pop to the shops to make sure I had Coco-Pops tomorrow... And he followed me.

Jen: To the shops?

Ben: Correct. I didn't really mind because I figured he could help me carry all the boxes of Coco-Pops to the checkout.

Jen: And did he?

Ben: No, he just ignored me and followed me around as I tried to balance six boxes of Coco-Pops all the way to the checkout. He didn't even help when I dropped a box right next to him.

Jen: How rude!

Ben: Very rude! In fact, I thought he might help carry the bags home, but no. He didn't help at all and that's what he's been like all day.

Jen: That's so strange.

Ben: Yep, he's just followed me around, not saying anything, not doing anything. Just following.

Jen: So, where is he now?

Ben: There, Jen.

Jen: Where?

Ben: Right there! Is there something wrong with your eyes? He's right there *[Ben points at his shadow]*.

Jen: Seriously, Ben? That's not a person following you around. That's your shadow!

Ben: Are you sure?

Jen: One hundred percent.

Ben: I thought he looked in good shape. Well, that's embarrassing.

Jen: I should think so.

Ben: I mean, you must feel really silly thinking my shadow was actually a real person. Jen, wouldn't it be really weird if someone was actually with you all the time but didn't do anything at all?

Jen: Yes, I can imagine that would be quite strange.

Ben: Come on Jen, let's go get some Coco-Pops.

Jen: I thought you'd already had breakfast?

Ben: First breakfast, Jen. First breakfast.

[Exit stage – Ben and Jen talking]

Ben: Hey Jen?

Jen: Yes, Ben?

Ben: Do you think One Direction will be coming back soon?

ACT ● PUPPETS

I CAN'T SEE GOD

Jack: Jill, Jill, I need your help.

Jill: You always need my help for something, Jack. What's going on?

Jack: Well, Alex said that God is always with us...

Jill: Yeah?

Jack: But I've been looking and I can't find Him anywhere!

Jill: Right?!

Jack: I've looked everywhere, I was thinking that He's proper good at hiding.

Jill: I suspect He is proper good at everything really – He is God.

Jack: I guess – but why would He hide?

Jill: Erm... well, have you looked in the cupboards?

Jack: Yep. Not there.

Jill: What about in the bathroom?

Jack: Yep. Not there.

Jill: The attic?

Jack: Not there.

Jill: Kitchen?

Jack: Not there.

Jill: *[Look left]* Over there?

Jack: He's not there.

Jill: *[Look right]* Over there?

Jack: He's not there.

Jill: He's BEHIND YOU!!

Jack: AGHHH! *[Turns around]*

Jill: He's BEHIND YOU AGAIN!

Jack: Where? What's happening?

Jill: He's over there!

Jack: I can't see Him...

Jill: Ooh, He's over there...

Jack: Why can't I see Him, what's going on? *[Spinning around all over the place]*

Jill: *[Laughing]* He's everywhere, Jack...

Jack: What? How can He be everywhere?

Jill: Because He's God! He is always with us because He's... are you ready for a big word?

Jack: I guess so.

Jill: Ahem... Omnipresent!

Jack: What's that mean?

Jill: God is omnipresent – He is everywhere all at the same time – we just can't see Him.

Jack: How does that work?

Jill: Well, I reckon you were looking for a person, weren't you?

Jack: Yeah, so?

Jill: Well, it's a bit tricky because our brains are very small...

Jack: Especially mine.

Jill: True. But God is not confined by our human definitions and understanding.

Jack: What?

Jill: God isn't like us. He's God. He can be everywhere all at once because He's *that* amazing.

Jack: Whoa!

Jill: He is omnipresent – that means wherever we go and whatever we do, God is right there with us.

Jack: So, He is behind me?

Jill: Yep.

[Exit – Jack and Jill]

Jack: And in front of me, too?

Jill: Yep.

Jack: I think I need a little lie-down...

[Exit stage – Jack]

Jill: Bless him. He really does only have a brain the size of a pea... I wonder if it's green as well? *[Exit – Jill, still talking]* Or tastes like a pea? That would be weird. Jill, you're talking to yourself again. Sssh, don't tell anyone.

GOD PROVIDES

8

THEME

The main theme today
is **God provides.**

God is good, and He loves to give us good things... Today we think about how God provides good things for us everyday.

STORY

This part of the story of Elijah is **amazing.**

God sends Elijah to tell Ahab that there will be no rain until he says, and then God sends him off to keep him safe during this drought, ironically to a place, which is called 'drought'! He then sends him to a widow who has nothing and He then sends him up to have a battle with some false prophets.

At every stage God is with Elijah and God provides whatever it is that he needs, whether it is water, food, a miracle, fire or calmness for Elijah. **God knows best, and God provides.**

IDEAS

This would be a great service to use for a **Harvest** service in your church.

Why not use this theme as another excuse to **have a meal together after church?**

ORDER OF SERVICE

3 MINS INTRODUCTION / WELCOME

3 MINS **SING** *Everybody's Welcome*

2 MINS **PRAY** Psalm 66: 1-2

3 MINS

SING
*All Things Bright
And Beautiful*

CREATE
Paint
God's provision

3 MINS **CREATE** Bird

10 MINS **ACT** *Elijah*

SCRIPT *see page 133*

2 MINS **TELL 1** God provides in mysterious ways

SCRIPT
see page 129

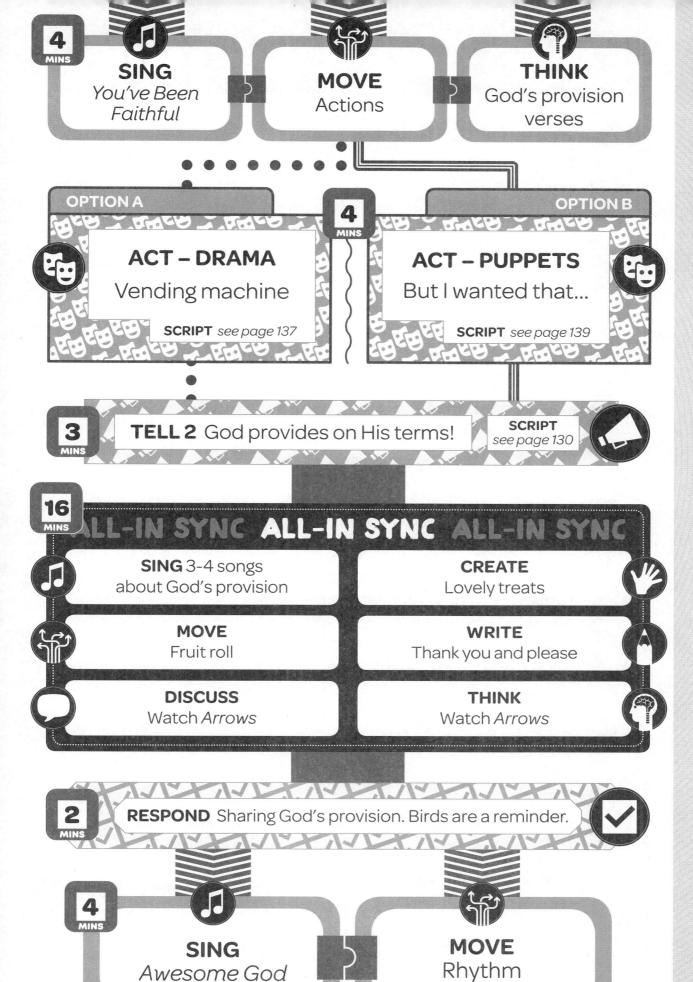

4 MINS

SING
You've Been Faithful

MOVE
Actions

THINK
God's provision verses

OPTION A

4 MINS

ACT – DRAMA
Vending machine

SCRIPT *see page 137*

OPTION B

ACT – PUPPETS
But I wanted that...

SCRIPT *see page 139*

3 MINS

TELL 2 God provides on His terms!

SCRIPT *see page 130*

16 MINS

ALL-IN SYNC ALL-IN SYNC ALL-IN SYNC

SING 3-4 songs
about God's provision

CREATE
Lovely treats

MOVE
Fruit roll

WRITE
Thank you and please

DISCUSS
Watch *Arrows*

THINK
Watch *Arrows*

2 MINS

RESPOND Sharing God's provision. Birds are a reminder.

4 MINS

SING
Awesome God

MOVE
Rhythm

THE FINER DETAIL

SING ▸ CREATE

SING

Lead the congregation in *All Things Bright And Beautiful** – with the new words, and preferably with a bit more of a rocky arrangement too, if you can!

All things bright and beautiful
All creatures great and small
All things wise and wonderful
The Lord God made them all

The seasons and the weather
The sun and moon and stars
The planets way beyond us
Like Jupiter and Mars

The little slug that slithers
The giant snail too
He made their boneless bodies
And covered them in goo

The creatures of the deep sea
The mountain-dwelling goat
To some He dished out fish-scales
To others furry coats

The leaping lime-green lizard
The slow and sleepy sloth
He set the speed they'd travel
Then smiled and set them off

He gave us eyes to see them
And lips that we might tell
How great is God Almighty
Who has made all things well

CREATE • Paint God's Provision

Provide an area with plastic sheeting on the floor and lots of paper and paint. Invite those who would like to, to paint a picture of God's provision to us to thank Him for that.

CREATE ◉ BIRD

The Easy Option Aeroplane birds

You need: A4 paper – one piece per person

Lead people in making a basic paper aeroplane, which they can pretend is a bird!

The Slightly Trickier Option Origami bird

You need: Squares of paper – one per person

Learn how to make the origami bird. Lead everyone in making the bird from their square of paper.

The Most Tricky (But Really Cool!) Option Slot-together bird

You need: Two strips of card per person
              Scissors
              Pens

Lead the congregation in shaping their rectangles into the shapes needed for making their bird.

They will need to cut slots in the pieces, which then slot together to make a three-dimensional bird!

 See www.bigministries.co.uk/theallinthing for tips, how to do all these **CREATE**s and help.

TELL 1 ● GOD PROVIDES IN MYSTERIOUS WAYS

God provided for Elijah in so many different, varied and fascinating ways.

There was a drought. God wanted to provide for Elijah and so He sent him to a place where He knew there would be water. This place was called the Kerith Ravine… Kerith means 'drought'. God has such a great way of showing how awesome His provision really is. He also sent birds to provide Elijah with food, and He chose to use the most ceremoniously unclean birds to do this – ravens. There was, in the eyes of the Jewish people, nothing good about ravens, and yet God used them to feed Elijah.

He then sent him to a widow who had nothing, and yet He provided for them both for the duration of the drought.

God provides, and in mysterious ways. Elijah trusted God even though He was sending him to a place called drought and to a woman who had nothing. Elijah trusted that God would look after him; God would provide… and He did.

Teach the congregation: **God provides in mysterious ways.**

See www.bigministries.co.uk/theallinthing for physical signs to teach the congregation.

SING ⬚ MOVE ⬚ THINK

SING

Lead the congregation in singing *You've Been Faithful****** – this song is on *The All-In Thing Songs* CD.

MOVE

 The actions for this song are on www.bigministries.co.uk/theallinthing.

THINK

Invite people to spend the duration of the song looking for Bible verses about God's

provision. Ideally, these verses should then be transferred up onto the screen (via tweet, text or hand-written notes!) for others to read.

TELL 2 ● GOD PROVIDES ON HIS TERMS!

God has promised He will always provide, and He will give good things to His children... but His provision for us may be different to how we think it should be. He absolutely knows best. Just think, Elijah probably thought, "what are you doing, God?" when God sent him to the Drought Ravine... But God knew what He was doing, and provided for him.

There's another element to God's provision too. Sometimes He wants us to get in on the provision for others, and for us to be His vehicle for providing for others. We have to be in tune with what He is doing to see what He wants of us, and demonstrate something of the good we have received to those around us.

Teach the congregation: **God wants us to help!**

See *www.bigministries.co.uk/theallinthing* for physical signs to teach the congregation to help them remember.

ALL-IN SYNC ALL-IN SYNC ALL-IN SYNC

SING

Sing a few songs about God providing for us.

Great Is Your Faithfulness
William M. Runyan, Thomas O. Crisholm

Psalm 23 (The Lord's My Shepherd)
Stuart Townend

We Plough The Fields And Scatter
Jane Montgomery Campbell, Johann Abraham Peter Schulz, Matthias Claudius

Yes God Is Good John H. Gurney

Praise God From Whom All Blessings Flow (Old 100th)
Louis Bourgeois, Thomas Ken

Tell Out, My Soul Timothy Dudley-Smith

Copyright details for songs can be found on page 156.

CREATE • Lovely treats

There's just one full idea here for this zone, but as long as you create something tasty for people, go for it. You could do sweets / no-bake cakes / anything you can think of.

Idea 1: Decorate Biscuits

You will need:

● Rich Tea biscuits

- Water icing
- Writing icing
- Sprinkles

Lead the zone in decorating biscuits for everyone, perhaps with messages of God's provision on them.

MOVE • Fruit roll

You will need:

- Fruit of differing shapes.

Sit the people in this zone in a circle. The aim is to try to roll the fruit to each other, as you receive the fruit, say thank you to God for something He has given us.

WRITE • Thank you and please

Write some thank you prayers.

Write some please prayers too.

In this zone, perhaps get details of any campaigns or petitions from Tearfund, Christian Aid or any other appropriate organisations, and have some of their publicity to fill in.

DISCUSS

Watch: Ethos *Arrows* (search for "Ethos Arrows" on Youtube).

God provides for us in so many ways – how can we show this to others by the way we act with them?

How can we provide for people in our community who need it?

THINK

Watch: Ethos *Arrows* (search for "Ethos Arrows" on Youtube).

God provides for us in so many ways – how can we show this to others by the way we act with them?

How can we provide for people in our community who need it?

RESPOND

Thank God for His amazing provision.

Ask Him to show us how we can provide for others who don't have as much as us.

Write or draw on your bird, something that you are going to do to show other people something of God's love and provision. Take the bird home as a reminder that you have committed to doing this.

SING MOVE

SING

Lead the congregation in singing *Awesome God**.

MOVE

Teach a few rhythms for people to do with their bodies (clapping / stomping) if they would like to. Lead these during the song.

 See *www.bigministries.co.uk/theallinthing* for help and details on this.

PRAY

It's not on the order of service, but do close the service with prayer!

ACT ● STORY
ELIJAH ● 1 KINGS 17-18

Characters:

- Narrator 1
- Narrator 2
- King Ahab
- Elijah
- Two Guards

- A person dressed as a Raven!
- A Woman and...
- ... her Son
- **You will need:**
- Two bulls (obviously not real ones)

---

*Teach the audience these **trigger words** before reading the story:*

Bad   *Say **"boooo"** with thumbs down.*

Good   *Say **"yeah!"** with thumbs up.*

Rain   *Say **"pitta-patta, pitta-patta"**, tapping fingers on lap.*

Raven(s)   *Say **"caw-caw!"** (your best impression of a raven).*

[Enter stage – Ahab]

Narrator 1: Ahab was far more evil than any of the kings that had gone before him. Anything that a person could do wrong, you name it, Ahab had done it.

Narrator 2: He was **bad**. Not **good**.

Ahab: That may be true, but there is no-one like me! No one greater than I! I am awesome!

Narrator 2: Ahab, you're a bit deluded aren't you?

Ahab: Firstly, you address me as, 'my Lord and King' and secondly... GUARDS! Seize this infidel! *[No response from any guards]* I said... GUARDS! Seize this infidel!... Where are they? Someone is losing their head over this... Just a minute.

[Exit stage – Ahab]

Narrator 1: Thankfully, there is someone else in this story. A man who was **good**. Not **bad**. His name was, Elijah.

Elijah: Hello. Elijah the Tishbite from Tishbe in Gilead here. Pleased to meet you.

Narrator 2: Elijah was one of God's prophets. God would speak to Elijah, and Elijah would deliver God's messages to the appropriate people. This time, Elijah had a message for Ahab.

[Enter stage – Ahab, with two guards]

Ahab: Right, let's try again... Aha! GUARDS! Seize this infidel! *[Pointing at Narrator 2 and then distracted by Elijah]* Erm, who are you?

[Guards stop and look confused, waiting for Ahab to continue with his order]

Elijah: Elijah the Tishbite from Tishbe in Gilead. And you must be Ahab.

Ahab: That's 'my Lord and King' to you.

Elijah: OK, whatever. I have a message for you from the actual Lord and King of Israel. The Lord God says that there will be no more **rain** or dew on this land except at my word.

Ahab: How dare you address me in this manner! Do you know who I am!? I am Ahab the Awesome! GUARDS! Seize this infidel!

[Elijah turns and runs off stage, closely chased by Ahab's angry guards, closely followed by Ahab]

Narrator 1: Having narrowly escaped the clutches of Ahab's men, Elijah then made his way to the Kerith Ravine, just as God had instructed him to.

> Someone could bring a paddling pool with a bit of water in, as a comedy-looking ravine.

[Enter stage – Elijah]

Elijah: Hello... Me again. Elijah the Tishbite from Tishbe in Gilead. God has told me that if I wait here, I can drink water from the brook and **ravens** will supply me with food... In actual fact, I'm starting to feel a little peckish right now.

[Enter stage – Person dressed as a Raven]

> It might be funny for someone to just wear a home-made raven beak and walk on as if they're annoyed at being picked for the part of the raven in the story. Little effort.

Narrator 2: Just then a **raven** flew in, dropping some bread and meat at Elijah's feet. And the same thing happened in the evening.

Elijah: Thank you, Mr. **Raven**.

Raven: You're welcome.

[Exit stage – Raven]

Narrator 1: Some time later, the brook had dried up because of there being no **rain** for some time.

Narrator 2: So Elijah got up, left the Kerith Ravine, *[exit stage – Elijah]* where he had been fed by **ravens**, and made his way to a place called, Zarephath, just as God had instructed him.

Narrator 1: Elijah finally arrived at Zarephath.

[Enter stage – Elijah]

Elijah: That was quick!

Narrator 2: Now, God had told Elijah that when he arrived in Zarephath he would meet a woman.

Elijah: Oh yeah! [*Thinking that he's being set up with a girlfriend*]

Narrator 2: No. Not like that. You'll literally just meet a woman.

Elijah: Oh... Hey, look! There's a woman gathering sticks. Just like God said there would be. [*Enter stage – woman*] Excuse me. Hello, I'm Elijah the Tishbite from Tishbe in Gilead. Could you bring me a little water in a jar so that I may have a drink... And some bread as well, please?

Widow: Sir, I can get you water but I don't have any bread. None! I only have a handful of flour and a little oil in a jar. I'm going to make my last meal for my son and I. We're going to eat it and then it wont be long until we die...

Narrator 1: This did not sound **good**. This sounded very, very **bad**.

Elijah: Don't worry. Go home and make me a small loaf of bread and then make something for yourself and your son, for the Lord God of Israel has said that your jar of flour will not be used up and your jug of oil will not run dry until God sends **rain** on the land again.

[*Person dressed as Raven runs across stage and the woman exits stage*]

Narrator 2: A **raven** flew past, and then the woman went away and did exactly as Elijah had told her. And so there was food everyday!

[*Enter stage – Woman and Son*]

Narrator 1: Some time later, the woman's son became really, really ill. So ill in fact, that he died! Obviously not **good**. Very, very **bad**.

> What might work well here is to use a puppet for the woman's son. The woman could walk on, holding the puppet.

Woman: [*To Elijah*] Why!? Why have you done this to me!? I look after you and God punishes me!?

Narrator 2: Elijah kept calm and did something that might appear to be a little odd. Well, in fact it did appear to be, and was, a little odd. Elijah stretched himself out over the boy's dead body three times and then shouted...

Elijah: My Lord God! Let this boy's life return to him!

Narrator 1: God heard Elijah's cry! Immediately the boy's life returned to him and he got up.

Widow: Thank you Elijah the Tishbite from Tishbe in Gilead. You really are a man of God.

[*Exit stage – Woman, Son and Elijah*]

> If you are short on time, you could end the story here.

Narrator 2: After all that drama, let's fast forward to the next part of our story, three years into the drought. Three years of no **rain**.

Narrator 1: God spoke to Elijah once again and told him to meet King Ahab. So, along with four hundred and fifty prophets of Baal and four hundred prophets of Asherah, Ahab met Elijah on top of Mount Carmel.

[*Enter stage – Ahab and Elijah*]

> You could have some people on stage as the prophets of Baal, dancing around and chanting like fools. Or invite some people from the audience up on stage to fulfill this coveted role!

Ahab: Elijah, you little troublemaker.

Elijah: Me? A troublemaker? You are the one making trouble. You've abandoned all of God's commands. You do whatever you want and worship lifeless, false gods. You are **bad**! You are far from **good**!

Ahab: How dare you! GUARDS! Seize the infidel!

Elijah: Hold on! I have a challenge for you.

Narrator 2: Ahab was intrigued and so Elijah then presented him and the people with the challenge.

Elijah: The challenge is – two Bulls placed on two different stacks of wood. One for you and one for me. You ask your gods to set your bull on fire. I'll ask my God to set my bull on fire. Whoever's god answers is the one true God. OK?

Ahab: Fine. Let the challenge begin.

Narrators 1: So, the prophets of Baal, who were **bad**, not **good**, prayed and shouted and did all sorts of things to get their god to set their bull on fire... but nothing happened.

Elijah: Time's getting on, guys. Maybe shout a bit louder. He could be sleeping.

Narrator 2: This went on for almost the entire day... Until...

Elijah: Enough! It's my turn.

Ahab: Arrrrgh. OK. Do your best Elijah.

Narrator 1: After making an altar and pouring twelve large jars of water over the bull and wood, Elijah prayed to God.

Elijah: Lord God! Let these people know that you are the one true God.

Narrator 2: Immediately, the bull and the wood and all of the water were consumed by scorching flames of fire.

Narrator 1: The people then fell with their faces to the ground and worshipped the one true God.

Narrator 2: And Ahab and the prophets of Baal ran...

Ahab: RUN!!

[Exit stage – everyone]

Narrator 1: After God had provided for Elijah throughout the entire drought, He then sent the **rain**. Which wasn't **bad**. It was actually really **good**.

Narrator 2: The end.

ACT ● DRAMA

VENDING MACHINE

After a quick game of tennis, Ben and Jen are thirsty and could do with a drink. *On spotting a vending machine, they pop their money in and expect to get the nice things that they ask for. However, the vending machine (which is a person dressed as a vending machine – work that one out) has other ideas and produces some vile products that are not helpful in the slightest to Ben and Jen's current needs. Thankfully, God is not like the broken vending machine in the sketch. God wants us to ask Him for good things and He wants to give us good things. See* **Luke 11: 1-13.**

You will need:

- A large box, turned into a vending machine, that a person can fit inside of.
- Coins
- A milk bottle
- A brick
- A large toy spider (or rat, or snake)

[Enter stage – Jen and Ben (looking sporty)]

Ben: That was a great game of tennis, Jen. You've improved.

Jen: I know. That's why I beat you.

Ben: You did not beat me. I won.

Jen: Only because I let you… So, really, I won… Hey look, a vending machine. What do you want? Chocolate? Crisps?

Ben: Chocolate crisps? No thanks. I'll just have a bottle of water.

Jen: OK. One bottle of water, coming up. Insert money, choose water, press button and there we have it…

[Vending machine hands over a bottle of gone-off milk]

Jen: What is this? This isn't water… It's white.

Ben: Hold on, it says here, 'semi-skimmed milk.' Not so bad… Dated October 2005… Hmm. *[Opens lid, smells milk… Drinks a little… Spits it out]* Well, that's not what I wanted. Where's my water?

[Ben shakes the vending machine to try to get his bottle of water]

Jen: You have a go. Maybe I pressed the wrong number.

Ben: I'll try something else. A sandwich, maybe. Oooh, look at that. My favourite! An all-day breakfast sandwich! OK, I'll just pop my money in here, choose the sandwich, press the button and…

[Vending machine produces a brick]

Jen: That looks like a brick.

Ben: It is a brick… I think. *[Pretends to bite brick]* Yep, it's a brick. Great. Maybe I'll be able to smash into the vending machine with it and get what I want.

[Ben raises the brick, ready to smash the vending machine]

Jen: No! Ben, you can't do that. That would be 'vender'-lism. We don't want to get in trouble. Look, we've tried to get some water and we get gone-off milk. We tried to get some food and we get a brick. Maybe this vending machine just doesn't deal too well with food and drink?

Ben: Good point. Hey, let's get one of those cuddly toys to cheer someone up. Look at them little, cute, cuddly bears.

Jen: OK. Insert money, choose cuddly bear, press the button and… ARRRRGH!!! *[Jen jumps into Ben's arms]* It's a sp-sp-sp-sp-spider! A GREAT BIG SPIDER!

Ben: What kind of vending machine is this? You ask for nice, good things and… and it gives you the complete opposite!

Jen: A spider…

Ben: *[Chucking Jen off him]* Relax, Jen. It's only a spider. I'm going home to get a drink.

[Exit stage – Ben]

Jen: Me too. *[Jen kicks the vending machine. The vending machine then begins following Jen]* Ben, the machine's following me. Ben… BEN!!

[The vending machine runs after Jen as Jen runs off petrified]

ACT ● PUPPETS

BUT I WANTED THAT...

Jill: *[Singing]* We plough the fields and scatter the good seed on the land.

Jack: I don't like that song, Jill.

Jill: Neither do I.

Jack: Well why are you singing it then?

Jill: Because it's Harvest. You have to sing that song at Harvest. It's like sprouts at Christmas. No-one really likes them.

Jack: I've never ploughed a field. Or scattered the good seed. But I did bring a tin of rollmop herrings for the Harvest collection.

Jill: 'Use by December 2008'?

Jack: How did you know?

Jill: Because I am so clever. Compared with you.

Jack: Jill, I'm terribly confused today.

Jill: You mean more so than usual?

Jack: Even more so than usual, yes.

Jill: Well, I'm sure I can provide an answer to your problem. Ask away, and ask me now.

Jack: Well, at Harvest we remember that God provides, right?

Jill: Right.

Jack: Provides us with things that we ask for, right?

Jill: Right.

Jack: Except that He doesn't.

Jill: Right. Wait, what?

Jack: Because I asked Him for a Ferrari last week and I still don't have one!

Jill: Jack, you are not old enough to drive. And how would you operate the pedals?

Jack: With my feet. *[Pause]* I still want a Ferrari.

Jill: Well, luckily for you, I know exactly where you're going wrong.

Jack: Oh yes?

Jill: You're not asking hard enough.

Jack: Eh?

Jill: Yeah, you need to ask God really, really hard.

Jack: Really, really hard?

Jill: Yeah. Screw up your eyes. Really think about the Ferrari and ask God in a really loud voice.

[*Jack follows the advice, making squeaking sounds and shaking with the effort of asking really hard*]

Jack: [*Shouting*] I WANT A FERARRI!

Jill: Please.

Jack: [*Louder still*] I WANT A FERRARI, PLEASE GOD!

Alex: Woah Jack, what's all this shouting?

Jack: Hi Alex. I prayed to God for a Ferrari and He didn't give me one so Jill said I had to ask really, really hard to show God I really, really wanted it and shout and then He would give me one.

Alex: You're not old enough to drive.

Jill: [*Smug*] That is exactly what I said.

Jack: I suppose a Lamborghini would do.

Alex: You know, Jack, I don't think Jill has got this one quite right, I'm afraid.

Jill: Well, I hadn't quite finished explaining it yet, actually.

Alex: Jack, have you got a house to live in?

Jack: Yes.

Alex: And some food to eat?

Jack: Yes. But no rollmop herrings.

Alex: And friends and family that love you?

Jack: Yes I have all those things.

Alex: Well maybe you should say thank you for the things God has already given you.

Jill: That is what I was going to say.

Jack: But why did God ignore me when I asked Him for a Ferrari?

Alex: Do you really need a Ferrari, Jack?

Jack: Well, I guess not. I mean, I'm not really old enough to drive.

Alex: God loves to give us good things, but He knows better than we do what is good for us and what isn't good for us.

Jill: So should we not ask God for anything?

Alex: God loves to hear from us, and it's great to ask Him for what we want. We just have to trust that He knows when to say yes and when to say no.

Jack: Maybe I should go and say thank you to God for my lovely bicycle, then.

Alex: That is a very good idea.

[*Jack and Jill begin to leave*]

Jill: Are you good at cycling, Jack?

Jack: Extremely good. Especially downhill.

REMEMBER

9

THEME

The main theme today is about **remembering**... and particularly **remembering God is good.**

When things are tough we can all too easily get stuck in a 'woe is me' frame of mind, when actually we need to hold onto the facts – **God is good,** He always has been and He still is, even if we can't feel it now. **We must remember.**

STORY

Joshua and the Israelites went through some **challenging stuff** together. The story in this session was not an unchallenging time!

Joshua knew that when life gets tough, and it feels like God is distant, it's good and important to **remember the good things God has already done for us** – this can help us get through the tougher times.

At the end of the story Joshua builds an altar. He builds this altar simply by stacking up a pile of stones next to where God has been doing amazing things, to help people **remember these amazing things** in the future! (This rock pile is sometimes called a **cairn**.)

IDEAS

You could definitely use elements of this service in a **service of Remembrance.**

You would need to include some of the more traditional elements of a Remembrance service, and also make space for the two-minute silence, so **be flexible.** (Maybe provide pipe cleaners or tangle toys to help those who struggle to be silent for that time!)

During the week leading up to this service, get someone with a camera to visit midweek groups and find out people's **first memories.** Collate these into a short video to then show in Tell 1.

ORDER OF SERVICE

3 MINS INTRODUCTION / WELCOME

3 MINS **SING** *Everybody's Welcome*

2 MINS **PRAY** Psalm 33: 1-3

4 MINS **SING** *Lord, For The Years (Lord Of The Years)*

MOVE Build a wall

3 MINS **CREATE** Memory stone

9 MINS **ACT** *Joshua*
SCRIPT *see page 148*

3 MINS **TELL 1** Remember – God is good
SCRIPT *see page 144*

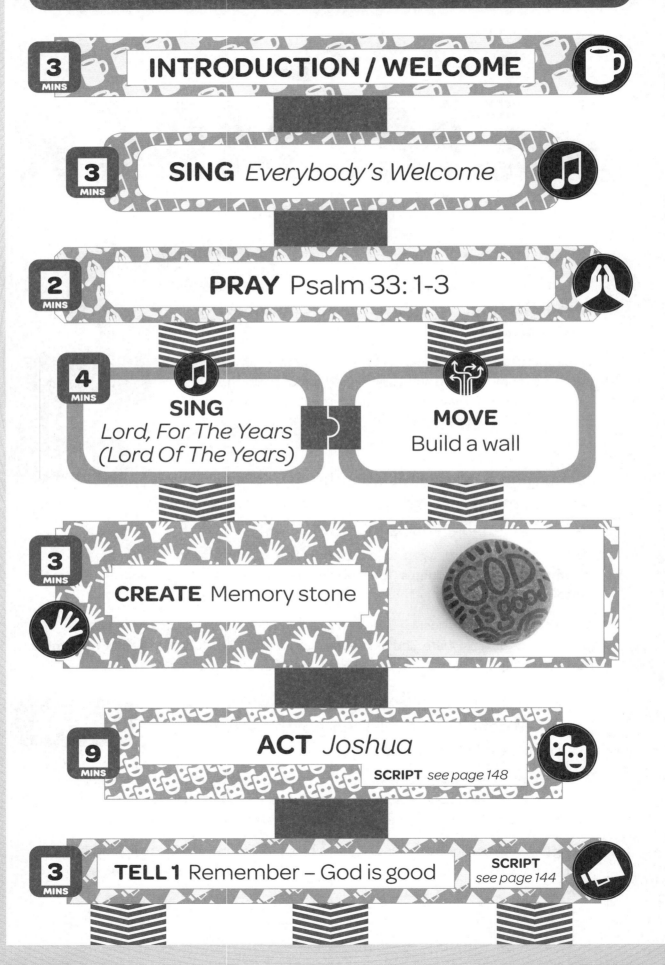

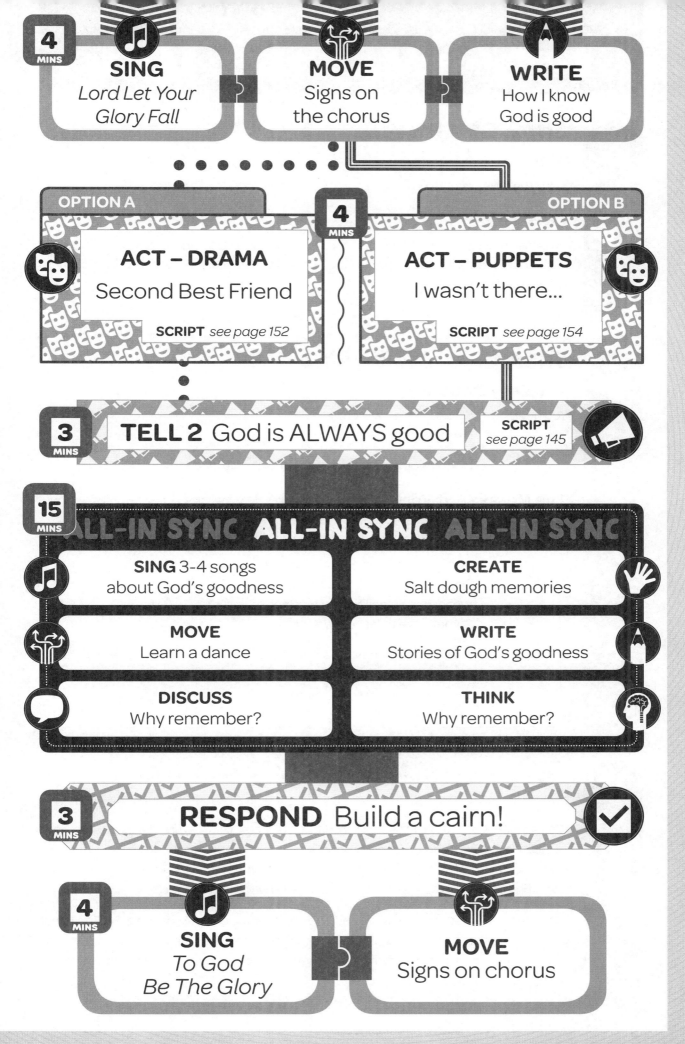

4 MINS

🎵 **SING**
*Lord Let Your
Glory Fall*

MOVE
Signs on
the chorus

WRITE
How I know
God is good

OPTION A

ACT – DRAMA

Second Best Friend

SCRIPT *see page 152*

4 MINS

OPTION B

ACT – PUPPETS

I wasn't there...

SCRIPT *see page 154*

3 MINS

TELL 2 God is ALWAYS good

SCRIPT
see page 145

15 MINS

ALL-IN SYNC ALL-IN SYNC ALL-IN SYNC

🎵 **SING** 3-4 songs
about God's goodness

CREATE
Salt dough memories

MOVE
Learn a dance

WRITE
Stories of God's goodness

💬 **DISCUSS**
Why remember?

THINK
Why remember?

3 MINS

RESPOND Build a cairn! ✓

4 MINS

🎵 **SING**
*To God
Be The Glory*

MOVE
Signs on chorus

THE FINER DETAIL

SING ▸ CREATE

SING

Lead the congregation in singing *Lord, For The Years******.

CREATE

Provide an area with building materials and Post-it notes – invite people who would like to, to build a wall, and to write attributes about God on the Post-its and stick them on the bricks.

CREATE ◉ MEMORY STONE

The Easy Option

You need: Stones – one per person
Permanent markers

Invite people to write "God is good" on their stone, or to colour it in.

The Messy (But Very Cool!) Option Clay bricks

You need: Mats / trays – one per person
Air-drying clay
(optional – pieces of wood for shaping the sides of the bricks)
Plastic 'tools'
Wet wipes or facilities for washing hands
Somewhere to leave the 'stones'

Lead people in making a brick with their lump of clay. Make them as rectangular as you can. Invite people to write into the top "God is good", or to draw something that symbolises God's goodness.

TELL 1 ◉ REMEMBER GOD IS GOOD

Show the 'first memories' montage (see "ideas" on the *Remember* introduction page).

It's a challenge for us to try and remember the first thing we remember – we have to search for methods of finding our way back in our minds! Remembering is a really powerful thing to do, because it brings back emotions and feelings and even sometimes smells or tastes that are associated with that memory.

In the story we just heard, Joshua saw the importance of remembering. He knew that at that moment the Israelites knew God was good, and they were in a place of praise because God had just literally rescued them and taken them through a river without getting them wet!

Joshua also knew that it wouldn't take long for the Israelites to forget this feeling, to forget how good God is when they are back in a place of despair and God feels distant.

So Joshua built an altar – a tower of stone to help people remember the amazing things God has done.

The sign for remember is like you are gathering your thoughts, grabbing them and locking them in a safe place... And that's what we want to do. God is good, and we have to remember that. We need to figure out a way of remembering... And do it!

Teach the congregation: **Remember... God is good.**

 See *www.bigministries.co.uk/theallinthing* for physical signs to teach the congregation.

SING MOVE WRITE

SING

Lord Let Your Glory Fall *****.

MOVE

Signs for chorus.

WRITE

"How I know God is good..." Make a list of how you know God is good.

TELL 2 ● GOD IS ALWAYS GOOD

God is good. He always has been good (we can see from stories in the Bible for a start), He IS good now, and He always will be good.

God is not just going to change to be something other than good and loving. Even when we're going through challenging times and it doesn't feel like God is good, we can know that He is good.

Let's share stories of what God's doing, let's encourage each other with how God is working. Let's help each other to not even have to 'remember' God's goodness... But have it at the forefront of our minds.

Teach the congregation: **God is ALWAYS good.**

See *www.bigministries.co.uk/theallinthing* for physical signs to teach the congregation to help them remember.

THE FINER DETAIL REMEMBER

SING

Sing a few songs about God's goodness and provision.

Water You Turned Into Wine
Matt Redman, Jonas Myrin, Chris Tomlin, Jesse Reeves

Good Forever
Jason Ingram, Matt Redman, Reuben Morgan

Copyright details for songs can be found on page 156.

CREATE • Salt dough memories

You have two options:

You can *make up the salt dough before the service* and then allow people to make their own memory object – this could be a handprint in a flat piece of salt dough or a three-dimensional shaped 'memory' or anything people can think of. Provide straws (for making holes to turn the object into an ornament) and tools (for shaping), and even ribbon to hang ornaments with.

Leave them to air-dry, or instruct people to take them home and bake them in a cool oven until hard.

OR

You could provide the flour, salt, water (and plenty of floor coverings!) and *making the dough could be part of the* **CREATE** *zone...*

MOVE • Dance

Find someone in the church who could make up a simple dance (preferably to a song), and who could then teach the people in this zone in learning and remembering it.

You could ask them to chat a bit about how they are trying to remember the moves, and what makes it easier / harder to do so.

WRITE • Stories

Provide paper, pens, envelopes and a shoe-memory-box.

"Write a story of God's goodness."

Seal the story in an envelope and put it in the 'memory-box'. This could be something that you then keep somewhere in the church and bring out in a year's time, or something to remind people of God's goodness when the church is going through a tough time.

DISCUSS

Have someone to lead the discussion.

Why is remembering so good?

What can we do to help us remember?

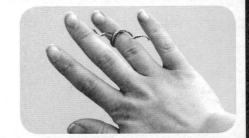

ALL-IN SYNC ALL-IN SYNC ALL-IN SYNC

What things should we forget?

Does God remember everything? Would it make Him not all-knowing if He forgot things?

THINK

Why is remembering so good?

What can we do to help us remember?

What things should we forget?

Does God remember everything? Would it make Him not all-knowing if He forgot things?

RESPOND

Thank God that He is good.

Build your own 'cairn' with the stones / bricks you made earlier in the service.

You could even build this outside as a permanent feature.

SING ▶ MOVE

SING

To God Be The Glory* – this song is on *The All-In Thing Songs* CD.

MOVE

Signs on chorus.

▶ See *www.bigministries.co.uk/theallinthing* for help and details on this.

PRAY

It's not on the order of service, but do close the service with prayer!

ACT ◉ STORY
JOSHUA ◉ JOSHUA 3-4

Characters:
- ◉ Narrator 1
- ◉ Narrator 2
- ◉ Joshua
- ◉ Israelite 1
- ◉ Israelite 2
- ◉ Stage hands
- ◉ Two Levitical Priests
- ◉ God

You will need three cue cards:
- ◉ SING
- ◉ RIVER
- ◉ PROMISES

And:
- ◉ Two people to hold the cue cards

You will also need:
- ◉ A tent
- ◉ Large length of blue material
- ◉ Two A3 signs, which read 'x6'
- ◉ Cardboard cutout of a bridge
- ◉ Cardboard cutout of a boat
- ◉ Twelve stones

Teach the audience the responses to the **cue cards** *before reading the story:*

[SING]	*Because the Israelites are camping, it would be the opportune moment to sing a camp fire song. We can't think of anything better than everybody's favourite. It is of course...* **"Kum-ba-ya, my Lord, kum-ba-ya!"**
[RIVER]	*Say* **"'Splish splosh splash!"**
[PROMISES]	*Shout* **"God always keeps His promises!"** *as fast as you can.*

Narrator 1: The Israelites had travelled to the River Jordan **[RIVER]** and were setting up camp... **[SING]**

[Enter stage – Israelites 1 and 2]

Israelite 1: *[Arguing whilst unsuccessfully setting up a tent]* No! That's not the centre pole! This one is.

Israelite 2: No, this one is! I've put this tent up more times than you've walked around a desert...

[Israelites 1 and 2 continue setting up the tent and squabbling (silently) whilst the narrators narrate]

Narrator 2: Once they had set up their tents and had a little sing-song **[SING]**, the Israelites awaited Joshua's instruction. Were they going to cross over the River Jordan? **[RIVER]** Would they ever enter the promised land? **[PROMISES]**

Israelite 1: Hurry up... the tent should be up by now.

Narrator 1: Were they going to be stuck here for days? Weeks? Years!? After all, they'd been travelling to this land for over forty years so far. Would they ever enter the promised land? **[PROMISES]**

Narrator 2: One day passed by...

Narrator 1: Two days passed by...

[Enter stage – Joshua]

Narrator 2: And after three days, Joshua sent an order out amongst the Israelite camp.

Joshua: Time to pack up and get ready to cross the River Jordan, ready to take the City of Jericho...

Israelite 1: *[Squashing tent into a bundle]* You're useless!

Israelite 2: Chill out... I've got feelings.

Joshua: At the precise juncture at which you yourselves do observe the Levitical Priests advancing forth with the Ark of the Covenant, you must proceed in your advancement towards the river **[RIVER]** in accordance with the given directive... that being that the extent of the distance between you and the Levitical Priests must be at least two thousand cubits.

Israelites 1 and 2: Huh?

Narrator 1: What Joshua means by that is, when you see the priests walking towards the river, carrying the Ark of the Covenant...

Narrator 2: ... That's a large box that contains the Ten Commandments and is a symbol of the Israelites' and God's promises to one another... FYI (For Your Information)...

Narrator 1: ... You are to follow them, but keep a distance of nine hundred metres...

Israelites 1 and 2: Oh!

Joshua: Did I not just say that?

[Exit stage – Joshua]

Narrator 2: And so, while squeezing in a few more good old campfire songs **[SING]** the people packed up camp and *[Enter stage – Levitical Priests.]* when they saw the Priests heading towards the river, they followed, keeping a distance of nine hundred metres...

Israelite 1: Quick, there they go. Let's follow...

[Exit stage – Israelites 1 and 2]

> It might look and sound good if Joshua used a megaphone to announce his orders... If you can get hold of one.

[Enter stage – The River Jordan (this is a couple of stage hands stretching some blue material from centre back to centre front of stage)]

Narrator 1: Now, it was harvest time. This meant that the River Jordan was at flooding level. **[RIVER]**

The people who are holding the blue material for the river could also be dressed in blue and have water pistols... What they do with them is your responsibility!

Narrator 2: There were thousands of Israelites that needed to cross, including children and babies...

[Enter stage – Israelite 1 with a large cardboard cutout of a bridge]

Narrator 1: There were no bridges...

[Exit stage – A disappointed Israelite 1 with bridge]

[Enter stage – Israelite 2 with a large cardboard cutout of a boat]

Narrator 2: and there were no boats...

[Exit stage – A disappointed Israelite 2 with boat]

Narrator 1: How on earth would they get across the river? It seemed as though they would never enter the promised land? **[PROMISES]**

Narrator 2: Maybe they should just give up and go back to sitting in their tents singing campfire songs **[SING]**. It seemed impossible.

Narrator 1: Thankfully, with God helping them, nothing was impossible. The priests approached the River Jordan, and as soon as their feet touched the water's edge, something absolutely incredible happened.

[Whoever is holding the back end of the blue material (The River Jordan) now needs to gather it all up into their arms so that it is no longer stretched across the stage]

Narrator 2: The water stopped flowing and gathered in a great heap up-stream, leaving an empty river bed for everyone to cross over to the other side.

[Enter stage – Joshua, followed by a barrage of Israelites]

Joshua: This way everyone. Keep moving. On to the City of Jericho and the land that God has promised us. **[PROMISES]** We're nearly there!

Narrator 1: When the whole nation of Israel had crossed over the River Jordan, God spoke to Joshua.

[Exit stage – Everyone apart from Joshua and two priests who remain stood in the middle of the river]

God: Joshua!

Joshua: Yes, Lord?

God: I want you to choose twelve men, one from each tribe, and tell them to pick up twelve stones from the middle of the river, where the priests are stood. Carry them with you and lay them down at the place where you stay tonight.

Narrator 2: So, Joshua did as God commanded and chose twelve men.

[Enter stage – Israelite 1 and 2 each with a large label pinned to their front, which says 'x6', meaning that Israelites 1 and 2 each represent six people]

Joshua: You twelve! Each of you is to go to the middle of the river, where the priests are stood, lift a stone upon your shoulders and bring it back. These will be a reminder to Israelites, for all time, that God cut off the flow of the River Jordan so that we could cross.

At this point in the story, instead of having the labels pinned to Israelites 1 and 2, you could choose ten people from the audience to collect a stone from the middle of the river, along with Israelites 1 and 2.

Narrator 1: So each of the twelve men from each of the twelve tribes of Israel went and got a stone from the middle of the River Jordan. **[RIVER]**

Israelite 1: Is he sure he wants a stone? I've just found a trolley...

Israelite 2: Yeah... Well, I've found a bike...

Israelite 1: Maybe we should just take a stone, like he said.

Israelite 2: Good idea... No way, a car!...

[Exit stage – Israelites 1 and 2]

Narrator 2: And so, once all twelve men were back from the middle of the river, Joshua called the Priests, who were carrying the ark, to come out from the middle of the river.

Joshua: Priests! You can come out now.

Narrator 1: And as soon as the Priests came out of the river, God allowed the waters to rush back down stream and return to normal. **[RIVER]**

[Blue material spreads down the middle of the stage again.]

[Exit stage – Levitical Priests]

Narrator 2: Night then began to fall and the Israelites, who were once again camping and singing **[SING]**, this time at a place called, Gilgal, just North of Jericho, were preparing themselves for the following day...

Narrator 1: ... The day when God would give them the City of Jericho, and following that, the entire land of Canaan, just as He had promised long ago. **[PROMISES]**

[Joshua sets up the stones in a pile]

Narrator 2: Meanwhile, Joshua set up the twelve stones from the river **[RIVER]** so that the people would always remember what God had done for them.

ACT ● DRAMA

SECOND BEST FRIEND

[Enter stage – Ben]

Ben: Oh good, I was hoping you'd all be here. I wish to notify you that I am advertising for the position of my Second Best Friend. Please just raise a hand if you are interested in a copy of the person specification and job description. Don't be shy, just raise a hand. *[To someone with their hand up]* Erm, no, if you could just pop your hand back down again...thanks. I must say that, whilst this is largely a voluntary role, there are certain social benefits and there is scope for promotion within my friendship group, pending the outcome of my number-one-best-friend Jen's annual appraisal. Between you and me, it's not looking terribly good for her right now.

[Enter Jen]

Ben: Oh, hi Jen. We were just talking about you.

Jen: All good things, I hope.

Ben: Well, really that's just between me and the potential applicants here.

Jen: Potential applicants?

Ben: Yes, potential applicants.

Jen: Applicants for what?

Ben: Applicants for the role of my Second Best Friend.

Jen: What happened to Duncan? I thought he was your Second Best Friend.

Ben: Nothing's happened to him. It's just that his performance as a friend is looking like it might be going down hill, that's all.

Jen: Oh dear, in what way?

Ben: Well, I'm concerned he might not get me a very good birthday present this year.

Jen: What? Duncan gives the best presents! Remember last year he managed to get you a copy of that game *Speed Racing Granny: New York City 3* when everywhere had been sold out for months. You said it was literally the best present anyone had ever given you.

Ben: I guess you're right... but I think he might start breaking promises.

Jen: What? Not Duncan. Duncan always keeps his promises. If Duncan says he will be somewhere, Duncan will be there. If Duncan says he will do something, Duncan will do it. If Duncan makes a promise, Duncan will...

Ben: *[Interrupting]* I get the point, Jen. Duncan keeps his promises... But I'm also a little worried he might start saying mean things about me and laughing at me behind my back.

Jen: What? Duncan is the most loyal person I know! Remember the other week when everyone laughed at you for wearing a T-shirt with a unicorn on the front?

Ben: No... I don't see what was so funny...

Jen: Well, Duncan stood up for you and the next day he wore a unicorn T-shirt so that people would make fun of him instead.

Ben: Well, I guess so... But I still don't understand why people found it funny. Unicorns are cool!

Jen: Hmm, I'm sure they are... Anyway, Ben, I think you're silly.

Ben: Watch it, Jen! You can be replaced like that *[clicks fingers]*.

Jen: OK, calm down. I just mean I think it's silly that you would think that Duncan is going to completely change who he is and start doing things that are completely out of character all of a sudden. It's like you have forgotten who Duncan is.

Ben: Jen, you have convinced me. Duncan truly is amazing. Let's go and find him so I can tell him how glad I am to have him as my Second Best Friend. Hey, I might even promote him...

[Exit stage – Jen and Ben]

Jen: Well, let's not be too hasty. I mean Duncan's good, but he's not *Jen* good.

Ben: I don't know, Jen... you'll never be cool enough to wear a unicorn T-shirt.

ACT ● PUPPETS

I WASN'T THERE...

Jack: All this talk of remembering is a bit weird to me, Jill.

Jill: Why? Don't you have a memory?

Jack: Yeah, I can remember *[dreamy voice]* tasting my first food... And taking my first steps.

Jill: REALLY?!

Jack: No, of course not – I thought you were the clever one.

Jill: Oh.

Jack: You know I'm a pup-pet, yeah? Not a lot of food nutrition required... Also... Check out the leg situation...

Jill: Oh... Yeah... Sorry.

Jack: So, Alex keeps talking about remembering the good that God has done – but I wasn't there, I didn't experience it all, so how am I supposed to remember?

Jill: Well, I think, that maybe... Erm... We need to get some sort of time-travel machine, maybe that's what he means..

Jack: YES, of course! You are so clever. Then we can go back, be part of the stories in the Bible and then we'll be able to remember that God was good... And is still good today!

Jill: Right, so where do we get a time machine?

Jack: Hmmm... Well I heard Stephen Hawking say that all you need to time travel is a wormhole and a really, really fast rocket.

Jill: Ok. That can't be too hard to source.

Jack: Sauce? We need ketchup too? I think I've got some in the fr...

Jill: No! Source – as in 'get'!

Jack: What?

Jill: Forget it. I think we have worms in the garden.

Jack: So we just need to find one and dig up the hole.

Jill: Yep. Good.

Jack: Jill... How do we dig up the hole?

Jill: Erm... That does sound quite tricky to do... But, erm... My little brother has a rocket toy and I think that flies pretty fast, so we've got that.

Jack: Good, so I'll go and try to figure out digging up a wormhole without upsetting the worms, you go get the rocket.

Jill: Check. Meet you back here in ten.

Alex: Hello you two, what are you up to? You look like you're on a mission!

Jack: We're just building a time machine so we can go and be part of all the stories in the Bible.

Alex : OK.

Jill: Yeah, because we can't remember the stories because we weren't there.

Jack: Right, I'm going to get the wormhole.

Alex: Hold on a minute – as exciting as a time machine would be, I'm not sure it's necessary.

Jack: But you told us to remember, and we can't!

Alex: Of course you can – that's why we have the Bible.

Jill: Yeah, I knew that.

Jack: You were the one who suggested a time machine.

Jill: Ha, I was joking…

Jack: You so weren't.

Alex: We have the Bible so that we can read stories about God, and how He has done amazing things – it's really cool because then when we are struggling to know what God is like, or going through hard times, we can read stories in the Bible that help us remember how good He is, and what He is like.

Jack: Oh, I see.

Jill: So we don't need a time machine?

Alex: No, not really.

Jack: Aw, that would have been fun.

Alex: Well, just because you don't need a time machine to remember God's goodness – doesn't mean you can't build one anyway, just for fun.

Jill: Yesss. Let's go!

[Exit – Jack and Jill]

Jack: Where shall we go first?

Jill: Ooh, I quite fancy the Victorian era.

Jack: That's boring, how about the dinosaurs' time?

SONG INFORMATION FOR SECTIONS 8-10

8 GOD PROVIDES

All Things Bright And Beautiful (rewrite)
Words: Steve Squires • © 2009 Song Solutions
Daybreak (Admin. by Song Solutions
www.songsolutions.org)

You've Been Faithful Damian Herbert / Steve
Squires • © Song Solutions Daybreak (Admin.
by Song Solutions www.songsolutions.org)
CCLI# 6494052

Awesome God Rich Mullins • © 1988 BMG Songs,
Inc (Admin. by BMG Music Publishing)
CCLI# 41099

Great Is Thy Faithfulness William M Runyan /
Thomas O Chisholm • © 1923, Renewed 1951
Hope Publishing Company CCLI# 18723

Tell Out My Soul Timothy Dudley-Smith •
© 1961 Timothy Dudley-Smith (Admin. by Oxford
University Press) CCLI# 2402653

Psalm 23 (The Lord Is My Shepherd) Stuart
Townend • © 1996 Thankyou Music (Adm. by
CapitolCMGPublishing.com excl. UK & Europe,
adm. by Integrity Music, part of the David C Cook
family, songs@integritymusic.com)
CCLI# 1585970

We Plough The Fields And Scatter
Jane Montgomery Campbell / Matthias Claudius
• Public Domain CCLI# 2647133

Yes God Is Good John Hampden Gurney •
Public Domain CCLI# 988152

Praise God From Whom All Blessings Flow
Louis Bourgeois / Thomas Ken • Public Domain
CCLI# 56204

9 REMEMBER

Lord, For The Years Timothy Dudley-Smith •
© 1976 Timothy Dudley-Smith (Admin. by Oxford
University Press) CCLI# 3274952

Lord Let Your Glory Fall Matt Redman
• © 1998 Thankyou Music (Adm. by
CapitolCMGPublishing.com excl. UK & Europe,
adm. by Integrity Music, part of the David C Cook
family, songs@integritymusic.com)
CCLI# 2526728

Our God (Water You Turned Into Wine)
Chris Tomlin / Jesse Reeves / Jonas Myrin /
Matt Redman • © 2010 SHOUT! Music Publishing
(Admin. by HMTR Limited) : Said And Done
Music / sixsteps Music / Thankyou Music/
Vamos Publishing / worshiptogether.com songs
(Adm. by CapitolCMGPublishing.com excl. UK
& Europe, adm. by Integrity Music, part of the
David C Cook family, songs@integritymusic.com)
CCLI# 5677416

Good Forever Jason Ingram / Matt Redman /
Reuben Morgan • © 2013 Hillsong Music
Publishing (Admin. by HMTR Limited) : Said
And Done Music / sixsteps Music / Thankyou
Music / worshiptogether.com songs (Adm. by
CapitolCMGPublishing.com excl. UK & Europe,
adm. by Integrity Music, part of the David C
Cook family, songs@integritymusic.com) : Open
Hands Music / Sony/ATV Timber Publishing
(Admin. by Sony/ATV Music Publishing)
CCLI# 7000698

10 CHRISTMAS

O Come All Ye Faithful (Adeste Fideles)
C. Frederick Oakeley, John Francis Wade •
Public Domain CCLI# 31054

He Came Down Words & Music: Unknown /
Traditional Cameroon • © Unknown

Joy To The World George Frideric Handel /
Isaac Watts • © Public Domain CCLI# 24016

*Immanuel (From The Squalor Of A Borrowed
Stable)* Stuart Townend • © 1999 Thankyou
Music (Adm. by CapitolCMGPublishing.com excl.
UK & Europe, adm. by Integrity Music, part of the
David C Cook family, songs@integritymusic.com)
CCLI# 2733786

God With Us Graham Kendrick • © 1988
Make Way Music www.grahamkendrick.co.uk
CCLI# 30251

Immanuel (He Is Here)
Graham Kendrick • © 1979 Make Way Music
www.grahamkendrick.co.uk CCLI# 222825

You're The King And You Reign Carey Luce /
Geraldine Latty • © 2003 Thankyou Music
(Adm. by CapitolCMGPublishing.com excl. UK
& Europe, adm. by Integrity Music, part of the
David C Cook family, songs@integritymusic.com)
CCLI# 4001911

10

ALL-IN CHRISTMAS

THEME

It's Christmas!
Happy Christmas to you!

Our focus for today is
Emmanuel – God is with us.

STORY

It's Christmas...
What other story could we have?
It's got to be the **Nativity!**

But let's not forget the amazingness of this scene, that **God came to Earth** and was born to an unmarried couple, and born in a smelly, dirty place where animals lived. Being born is a messy deal... Jesus went through that because He wanted to come to Earth and live just as we live, to show us that **He truly is God with us.**

IDEAS

The week before this service, set the **challenge of the best Christmas selfie.** Get them emailed in, and then they can be rolling on the screen at the start of this service – a whole lot of fun.

This service could definitely be advertised as something non-threatening to invite people to. Get people in and make sure you offer mince pies / Christmas cake / chocolate log and **all the lovely treats we are allowed at Christmas!** You could even have mulled wine (non-alcoholic options are available) and chocolate coins, or something else delightful, for after the service.

ORDER OF SERVICE

3 MINS — **INTRODUCTION / WELCOME**

3 MINS — **SING** *Everybody's Welcome*

2 MINS — **PRAY** Psalm 66: 1-3

4 MINS

SING
*O Come
All Ye Faithful*

CREATE
Pipe cleaner
decorations

4 MINS — **CREATE** Angel

8 MINS — **ACT** *Jesus is born*
SCRIPT *see page 164*

3 MINS — **TELL 1** Jesus is God-con-carne
SCRIPT *see page 160*

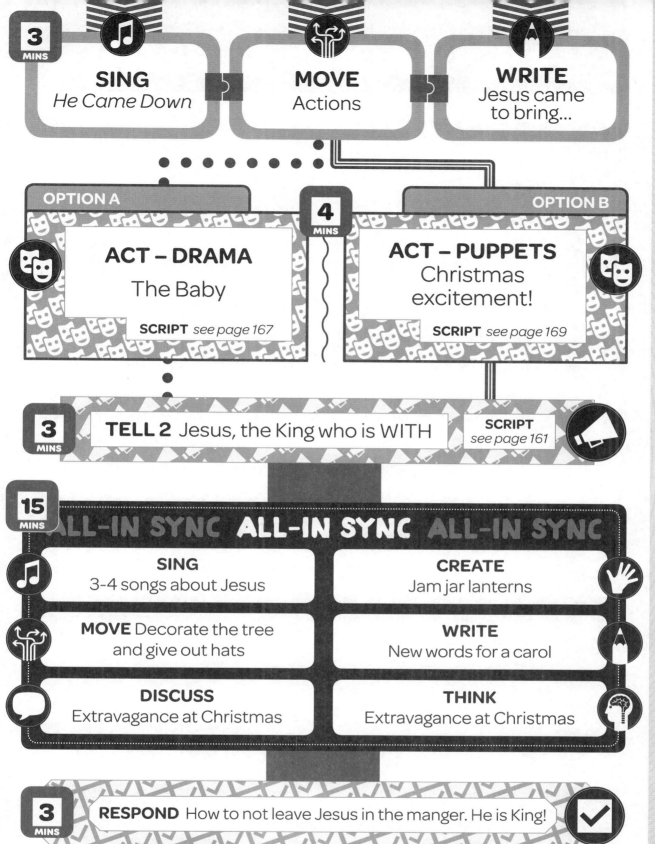

3 MINS

SING *He Came Down*

MOVE Actions

WRITE Jesus came to bring...

OPTION A

4 MINS

ACT – DRAMA The Baby

SCRIPT *see page 167*

OPTION B

ACT – PUPPETS Christmas excitement!

SCRIPT *see page 169*

3 MINS **TELL 2** Jesus, the King who is WITH

SCRIPT *see page 161*

15 MINS

ALL-IN SYNC ALL-IN SYNC ALL-IN SYNC

SING 3-4 songs about Jesus

CREATE Jam jar lanterns

MOVE Decorate the tree and give out hats

WRITE New words for a carol

DISCUSS Extravagance at Christmas

THINK Extravagance at Christmas

3 MINS **RESPOND** How to not leave Jesus in the manger. He is King!

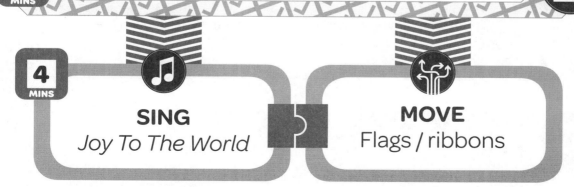

4 MINS

SING *Joy To The World*

MOVE Flags / ribbons

THE FINER DETAIL

SING CREATE

SING

O Come All Ye Faithful*- a great gathering carol!

CREATE

Provide pipe cleaners for those who would like to worship God by being creative – they can make a decoration for the tree with their pipe cleaner.

CREATE ◉ ANGEL

You will need a pipe cleaner and a piece of A6 paper for every person.

Make a fan out of the paper (lengthways) and then use the pipe-cleaner to be the angels head and a 'holder' for the angel... It's really tricky to explain, but easy to do. Watch the video!

 See *www.bigministries.co.uk/theallinthing* for how to do all this **CREATE**.

TELL 1 ◉ JESUS IS GOD-CON-CARNE

Bit of a weird question for you at this time of year, but who likes *chilli con carne*?

Me too! Now, I like it nice and spicy, with lots of chilli. Did you know the name *chilli con carne* literally means "chilli with meat". The word incarnate comes from the same heritage!

We say that Jesus was God incarnate. Literally this means that Jesus is God with meat on God — Jesus is God in human form.

Jesus is God WITH us. Jesus feels everything as we do, He lived, hurt, He got lost, He was cold and hungry, He fell over, He felt silly, He was excited, He was poorly. He was fully human.

He came down to bring us hope, love, life and joy. Jesus is God here on Earth.

Teach the congregation: **Jesus is God on Earth.**

See *www.bigministries.co.uk/theallinthing* for physical signs to teach the congregation.

SING MOVE WRITE

SING

He Came Down* – this song is on *The All-In Thing Songs* CD.

MOVE

 Actions – see *www.bigministries.co.uk/theallinthing* for actions.

WRITE

"Jesus came to bring..."

Invite people to write down things that Jesus came to bring. There are a few in the song, can we think of more? (You could then get some feedback and add them into the song.)

TELL 2 ● JESUS IS THE KING, THE KING 'WITH'

Has anyone ever met the Queen? Or anyone in a position of royalty?

It's rare, isn't it? And it's even more rare for you to be on first name terms with the Queen, and for her to come around for a cuppa and a slice of cake on a Tuesday afternoon!

Jesus was born as a King, our King; but the unique thing about His Kingship is that He is a King who is absolutely with us. He is Emmanuel – God with us.

Jesus could easily be a King who is different and separate from us (He is God after all!), but He is not a King like that. Jesus is not 'completely different' from us, He is not a King in a palace with His 'subjects' waiting on His every whim. He is the King who was born in a smelly animal house, grew up as a carpenter, and ultimately gave His life for His subjects. Jesus came to Earth to be the King, but the best sort of king – the King who lives with us, in our mess.

Teach the congregation: **Jesus is Emmanuel.**

 See *www.bigministries.co.uk/theallinthing* for physical signs to teach the congregation to help them remember.

ALL-IN SYNC ALL-IN SYNC ALL-IN SYNC

SING

Sing a few songs about Jesus – or a few carols if you'd rather!

Immanuel (From The Squalor Of A Borrowed Stable) Stuart Townend

Here I Am To Worship (Light Of The World) Tim Hughes

God With Us (He Walked Where I Walk) Graham Kendrick

You're The King And You Reign Carey Luce, Geraldine Latty

Immanuel (He Is Here) Graham Kendrick

Copyright details for songs can be found on page 156.

THE FINER DETAIL CHRISTMAS

CREATE • Jam jar Lanterns

You will need:

- Jam jars
- Tissue paper
- PVA glue
- Glitter
- Glo-sticks or tea lights
- Wire to make handles

Decorate the outside of the jar with ripped up tissue paper, glue and glitter.

Use the wire to wrap around the top of the jar and make a handle.

Insert 'light'!

MOVE • Decorate and distribute!

You will need:

- Decorations / things to make decorations with
- Party hats

Invite the Movers to decorate the church and to distribute party hats to everyone in the church.

WRITE • New carol

Re-write the words for an old Christmas carol!

Provide the words to some of the favourite carols in this zone so people have something to work from.

DISCUSS • Extravagance

God sending Jesus was an extravagant gift.

Do we show this sort of extravagance?

Does our extravagance have a lasting, positive impact or just a momentary impact?

How can we model extravagance like God?

THINK • Extravagance

God sending Jesus was an extravagant gift.

Do we show this sort of extravagance?

Does our extravagance have a lasting, positive impact or just a momentary impact?

How can we model extravagance like God?

RESPOND

How can we keep Jesus in His rightful place at Christmas time? Not in the manger, but as the truly amazing KING He is.

Write ideas on your crown and take it with you as a reminder.

SING ▶ MOVE

SING

Lead the congregation in singing *Joy To The World*.

MOVE

Time to bring out the flags and ribbons – or even tinsel to wave around! It is Christmas, after all!

PRAY

It's not on the order of service, but do close the service with prayer!

ACT ● STORY
JESUS IS BORN
MATTHEW 1: 18-25 AND LUKE 2: 1-16

Characters:
- Narrator 1
- Narrator 2
- Mary
- Joseph
- Angel
- Inn Keeper
- Shepherd 1
- Shepherd 2
- Shepherd 3

You will need four cue cards:
- AAAAH
- CHEER
- GASP
- HALLELUJAH

And:
- Two people to hold the cue cards

Teach the audience the responses to the **cue cards** *before reading the story:*

[AAAAH] **A soppy kind of "aaaah",** *not a scared-for-your-life "aaaargh!"*

[CHEER!] *Everyone* **cheers.**

[GASP] *A* **gasp** *of shock.*

[HALLELUJAH!] *Shout* **"Hallelujah!"**

Narrator 1: Mary and Joseph were in love. They were engaged and would soon be married.

[Enter stage – Joseph]

Joseph: I love Mary so much. I can't wait to be her husband and have children with her and be a dad. It's all so exciting. **[AAAAH]**

[Enter stage – Mary]

Mary: Joseph!

Joseph: Mary, my love. I was just thinking…

Mary: Joseph, I'm pregnant. **[CHEER!]**

[Joseph stares into space]

Mary: Joseph, did you hear me? I said, "I'm pregnant."

Joseph: With a baby?

Mary: Yes. With a baby.

Joseph: Oh... Erm... Wow, is that the time? I've just remembered this thing that I've got to do... Somewhere else... But not here. Definitely not here. Good night.

[Exit stage – Mary]

Narrator 2: That evening, Joseph tried to figure out a way that he could keep this whole thing quiet, and whether or not he would still stay with Mary, as he was pretty sure that he wasn't responsible for her pregnancy! **[GASP]**

> You could create a little room for Joseph on the stage, with a quilt and a bedside lamp.

Joseph: Unless what they taught me at school about the birds and the bees was a lie? We have held hands a couple of times. **[AAAAH]**

[Joseph lies down to sleep]

Narrator 1: But that night, an angel spoke to Joseph in a dream. **[GASP]**

[Enter stage – Angel]

Angel: Joseph. Take Mary as your wife. The child that she carries was put there by God's Holy Spirit. She will have a son, and you will name Him Jesus because He will save His people.

[Exit stage – Angel]

Narrator 2: As soon as the dream had finished, Joseph sat up, eyes wide open. He was in a state of shock at what he'd just been told by the angel. And also in a state of immense relief that everything now made sense... Kind of.

> Joseph could chuck a glass of water in his own face to wake himself up and come around from his state of shock.

[Exit stage – Joseph]

Narrator 1: While Joseph worked out how to balance these emotions, he and Mary made their way to Bethlehem, where Joseph's family were from, as there was a census taking place.

[Enter stage – Mary and Joseph. Mary is now heavily pregnant]

Mary: When can we stop travelling!?

Joseph: When we get to Bethlehem.

Mary: Thank you, Captain Obvious! Why don't you tell me something I don't know... Oh, Joseph, my love, I'm sorry... I'm just so massively pregnant. My emotions are everywhere.

Joseph: It's OK. I understand.

Mary: Oh. You understand, do you!? Do you really!? Have you ever carried a child inside you for months!? Have you!? HAVE YOU!?

Joseph: Look. There's Bethlehem. I recognise it. **[CHEER!]**

Narrator 2: Arriving in Bethlehem, Mary and Joseph struggled to find a room due to it being Christmas-time.

Joseph: What's Christmas-time?

Mary: Yeah, I've never heard of Christmas-time.

Narrator 1: Hmm, that can't be right. Christmas doesn't exist yet. Mary and Joseph struggled to find a room due to it being... the census.

> When Mary and Joseph arrive, you could play a Christmas song as if the town of Bethlehem were celebrating Christmas. Then stop the music as soon as it's mentioned that Christmas doesn't exist yet.

[Enter stage – Inn Keeper]

Joseph: Excuse me, sir. Have you got any idea where my wife and I can stay?

Inn Keeper: My, you're massive! **[GASP]**

Mary: It's called, 'being pregnant', Mr. Tactful.

Inn Keeper: Sorry. Look, everywhere is massively... I mean 'fairly' full up this week. Looks like this trip's gone belly-up for you. No, not 'belly', I mean this trip's gone 'wrong' for you. What you need is a huge, giant, large, rotund piece of pregnant belly luck... Sorry. I'm nervous. Don't hurt me. Sticky-out belly button.

Joseph: Look, do you know of anywhere we can stay? Anywhere at all?

Inn Keeper: OK. So, I do have a room, **[CHEER!]** but it's where the animals eat and sleep. **[GASP]** You're more than welcome to it.

Joseph: Thank you so much. We'll take it!

[Exit stage – Inn Keeper, followed by Mary and Joseph]

Narrator 2: And so, Mary, at some point during her stay in some of the most unsuitable accommodation in Bethlehem, had a baby; A baby boy who was named Jesus. **[AAAAH]**

[Enter stage – Shepherds)

Narrator 1: Soon after this, an angel of the Lord appeared to a group of shepherds who were out looking after their sheep.

[Enter stage – Angel]

Angel: Hey, everyone!

Shepherds: ARRRGHH!

Shepherd 1: Run!

Shepherd 2: Save yourself!

Shepherd 3: What have we done to deserve such terror!?

Angel: What's going on? Don't be afraid.

Shepherd 1: Oh. OK. Hey guys, he said don't be afraid.

Shepherd 2: Phew. I thought that was the end for a moment.

Shepherd 3: Anyone know where the nearest toilet is?

Angel: I just came to tell you that a baby has been born in Bethlehem. A very important baby.

Shepherd: We should totally go and worship that baby. **[CHEER!]**

[Exit stage – Shepherds and angel]

Narrator 2: And so, the shepherds left what they were doing in order to find where Jesus was.

Narrator 1: And when they found Him, they, along with a few other wise visitors, worshipped Him. They worshipped Jesus, the Son of God, born to change the world. **[HALLELUJAH!]**

> If you have some bright lights, you could shine them on the angel. You could also play a clip of the *Hallelujah Chorus* from Handel's *Messiah* when the angel appears.

ACT ● DRAMA

THE BABY

You will need:
- ◉ A large Nativity Scene or a toy baby in a manger on stage
- ◉ A bag of sweets

[Enter stage – Ben]

Ben: Christmas is ridiculous! There, I said it – the very thing everyone was thinking. Now, we can all forget about the whole pointless and ridiculous thing and get on with some sort of normality. You're welcome.

[Enter stage – Jen , looking around the room]

Jen: Uh-oh. I sense awkwardness. What have you said now, Ben? Seriously, your ability to make everyone in the room feel uncomfortable is truly astounding.

Ben: Thank you… And I was merely releasing everyone here from the shackles of the ridiculous thing we call Christmas.

Jen: Christmas isn't ridiculous. *[Jen offers Ben a sweet]* Humbug?

Ben: No, I'm fine thanks, and yes, Christmas is ridiculous. Think about what it's about. Firstly, it's about getting cut down trees and putting them in our houses and hoovering about nine times a day. Ridiculous!

Jen: That's not really what Christmas is about…

Ben: OK, well then it's all about singing weird songs about angels, farming folk and donkeys… And it's all going OK, then all of a sudden all the ladies snap for a verse and start singing insanely high. Then they just go back to normal as if nothing happened. Ridiculous!

Jen: Again, that's not really what Christmas is about…

Ben: Then it's all about buying an enormous turkey and cooking it for like a week or something and then… then… get together and you eat it! I mean, turkey… Who even likes turkey? No-one.

Jen: Yes, they do!

Ben: Oh yeah? Then how come no-one eats turkey at any other time of year?

Jen: Well, because… because…

Ben: Exactly. No-one likes turkey. Ridiculous.

Jen: Ben, I think you're really missing the point for a change. Those are just some of the ways in which we celebrate Christmas, but it's not what Christmas is about. Christmas is all about Jesus.

Ben: Oh, so we do all this stuff because of a baby! Oh, so that's not ridiculous?

Jen: But this baby was different.

Ben: *[Picking up Baby Jesus from the Nativity by the foot]* Doesn't look very different.

Jen: Erm, I'm not sure you're allowed to do that.

Ben: Babies don't even do anything except cry and eat and, *[ahem]* you-know-what. Babies are pretty much the most pointless things ever and Christmas doesn't make sense. Christmas is ridiculous!

Jen: Can we just put Baby Jesus back in the manger now before you offend someone... *[Jen takes the baby and places it back in the manger]*

Ben: You want to know the most ridiculous thing of all? People don't even seem to realise that babies don't stay babies. They grow up and some of them even have beards! Nope, it's ridiculous and I need to cancel it for everyone's benefit.

Jen: I'm not sure you have the authority to do that...

Ben: Ladies and gentlemen, I have an announcement to make – I am officially cancelling Christmas.

Jen: If you're cancelling Christmas then I guess you won't want the really nice present I bought you this year?

Ben: Ladies and gentlemen, I have an announcement to make – I am officially cancelling Christmas... Next year. I'm cancelling it next year.

Jen: Wow, there really aren't any hidden depths to you are there, Ben.

Ben: Nope, none whatsoever. So, Jen, tell me more about this present.

[Exit stage – Ben and Jen]

Ben: Is it big? Ooh, is it heavy? Do you have to plug it in? Tell me, tell me.

ACT ● PUPPETS

CHRISTMAS EXCITEMENT!

Jill: Hey Jack, I've got a question for you.

Jack: For me? I'm not very good at questions, but I'll have a go.

Jill: Are you ready?

Jack: I'm a bit nervous. You know I'm not as clever as you at questions.

Jill: Here is the question – what is the most exciting thing of all about Christmas?

Jack: I know this one! It's the presents, Jill. The presents are the most exciting thing about Christmas.

Jill: Jack, you hit the nail on the head, first time. You're not as stupid as you look.

Jack: Eh? What do you mean?

Jill: I mean, you are right. The presents are the most exciting thing about Christmas.

Jack: Really? The presents?

Jill: Really.

Jack: I'm a bit surprised to hear you say that, Jill. It's just that I'm not usually right.

Jill: Well, I have to give it to you, Jack. On this occasion you are spot-on.

Jack: So it's not the tree?

Jill: The tree?

Jack: Yeah, going to the garden centre and buying a great big tree. And bringing it home, finding it's much too big for your house and then covering it with shiny, shiny things that have been in the big, magical, dusty cardboard box in the loft since last Christmas.

[Pause]

Jill: Actually Jack, you're right, that is the most exciting thing about Christmas.

Jack: More exciting than the presents?

Jill: Even more exciting than the presents.

Jack: But what about the Nativity?

Jill: What about the Nativity?

Jack: I always thought doing the Nativity play at church was the most exciting thing about Christmas. Getting to dress up as a shepherd and stand around with a towel on my head holding a great, big, cuddly sheep and then seeing all those angels appear and then taking my sheep to see the newborn Baby Jesus.

[Pause]

Jill: Actually, that is pretty exciting too.

Jack: And then there's Christmas lunch; roast turkey, potatoes, sausages in blankets, gravy.

Jill: Sprouts...

Jack: The sprouts are not the most exciting thing about Christmas.

Jill: Oh, what about seeing all your family?

Jack: Oh yes, that too.

Jill: And baby Jesus being born.

Jack: Definitely. I think all those things are the most exciting thing about Christmas.

Jill: Jack, I agree with you. All those things are equally exciting and therefore the most exciting thing about Christmas.

Jack: I'm glad we agree, Jill.

[Enter stage – Alex]

Jill: Alex, I have a question for you – what is the most exciting thing about Christmas?

Alex: Well... Probably...

Jack: *[Interrupting]* I know you're going to say it's the presents. Well, that is one of the things, but there's lots of other things that are just as exciting; the tree, doing the Nativity play, remembering Baby Jesus being born, seeing your family, Christmas lunch. We agreed, Jill and I.

Alex: Oh, you agreed, did you?

Jill: Very much so.

Alex: Well, I'm not sure that I agree with you, I'm afraid.

Jack: But we agreed!

Alex: All those things are pretty exciting, but I think there is one thing that is more exciting than all the rest.

Jack: Christmas lunch?

Jill: Presents?

Alex: Jesus is the best thing about Christmas because without Jesus there is no Christmas. Jesus is Emmanuel, which means "God with us" here on Earth. Pretty amazing, really...

Jack: Alex makes a good point, Jill.

Jill: Hmm. Yes. It's basically what I said earlier.

Jack: No you didn't.

[Exit – Jack and Jill, still talking]

Jill: Well, I said it in my head.

Jack: I don't think you did.

Jill: Well... I did.